HOW TO BE

TO BE

hopeful

AN INSPIRATIONAL GUIDE TO
Ignite a Life FULL OF HOPE,
HAPPINESS, AND COMPASSION
FOR YOURSELF AND OUR FUTURE

Bernadette Russell

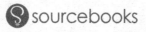

Published by Sourcebooks
P.O. Box 4410, Naperville, Illinois 60567-4410
(630) 961-3900
sourcebooks.com

Originally published in 2020 in Great Britain by Elliott and Thompson Limited.

Library of Congress Cataloging-in-Publication Data is on file with the publisher.

Printed and bound in the United States of America.
SB 10 9 8 7 6 5 4 3 2 1

contents

INTRODUCTION
in search of hope

"HOPE" IS THE THING WITH FEATHERS –
THAT PERCHES IN THE SOUL –
AND SINGS THE TUNE WITHOUT THE WORDS –
AND NEVER STOPS – AT ALL –

—EMILY DICKINSON

A YEAR AGO, I WAS ON the number 47 bus toward Lewisham in Southeast London, a pretty regular route for me, when I overheard a woman say to her friend, "The news made me cry this morning. I just wanted to go back to bed. Everything is so awful."

All that week, I couldn't stop thinking about what the woman had said. I began to pay greater attention to all the expressions of despair, pessimism, and cynicism that I heard from friends, family, neighbors, and work colleagues. I noticed so much of this online and in the news; it seemed to me as though a dark cloud hung over us all. As I watched and listened attentively, it appeared we were doing very little but talk about how awful everything was or else were sticking our heads in the sand and praying it would all go away. It looked like hope was an endangered species, and yet I couldn't see how things could possibly improve without it.

We live in a truly amazing world, despite the very real and present troubles we face, but it seems that many of us are struggling to find hope for ourselves, for our communities, or for the world at large. So many people have told me that they feel very bleak about the future, that they feel scared all the time, depressed, anxious, and powerless. Although we are sometimes still able to laugh, to find joy, it seems that lots of us are hemmed in by a quiet despair. I didn't want to simply passively accept that this was the way things were. I was determined to work out how to find hope and how to hold on to it. And I wanted to help everyone else to do so too. Hope feels like the basis from which all possibilities spring; without it, positive change just does not feel achievable.

The first time I can remember hearing a story about hope was when my Sunday school teacher Mrs. Hibdidge told me about Pandora's box. I think a lot of people will recall this tale, vaguely at least, but to recap: Pandora is given a box that she is told she must never open (yep, it's obvious where this is going). Inevitably, after a while, Pandora opens the box, and all at once, out fly all the evils of the world: grief, famine, death, greed, disease, anger, sorrow, pain—you get the picture.

Shocked, Pandora shuts the box, but the evils have bolted—it's too late. The earthly paradise is no more. After weeping in despair,

Pandora hears a faint cry from within the box, imploring her to open it again. Presumably, she decides that it probably can't get much worse, so she does.

Then out flies Hope—tiny, golden, plucky Hope—to protect humankind from all of the evils of the world. What Hope was doing in such bad company is a philosophical conundrum which has divided thinkers, writers, artists, and spiritual leaders since the story was first recorded in the eighth century BC. Some see Hope as a punishment, just another evil in the box—a false promise of better things to come that could only prolong our torment. Others have suggested Hope was placed there as a gift from the gods to help us in our times of need.

This is how I feel about hope today. To me, it's our main shield and weapon against the problems in the world. Hope allows us to believe that things can get better, helping us to find a way through our dark times. I am certain of this. So I was sad and frustrated to find such a disconnection from hope in our collective lives. Being hopeful does not come naturally to all of us—myself included. When times were tough (and they have been very tough), I had to fight to remind myself how important hope really is. I had to teach myself to look for it, to act on it, how to use it to make sure I kept on going. In time, it gradually became a habit. I've since found it easier to weather disappointment and to shrug off despair, to focus on the positives and the possibilities. There is always hope, you see.

One of the first things I discovered on this journey to hope was that I'm far from the first person to place upon it such a high value. The ancient Greek philosopher Aristotle thought that hope should be seen as a virtue, as it makes a person courageous, giving us the confidence that things will turn out well if we take action and the fear of what might happen if we do nothing. In the thirteenth century, the Catholic priest and philosopher Thomas Aquinas considered hope to be one of three Christian virtues, along with faith and love. He described it as a future good that was difficult but possible to attain, although he believed we needed God's help to achieve it. So in terms of believing in the vital importance of hope, I'm in pretty good company.

Of course, it has not always been seen as a positive thing. In 1878, the philosopher Friedrich Nietzsche argued for the alternative interpretation of the Pandora myth in his book *Human, All Too Human:* "Zeus did not want man to throw his life away, no matter how much the other evils might torment him, but rather to go on letting himself be tormented anew. To that end, he gives man hope. In truth, it is the most evil of evils because it prolongs man's torment."

What a buzzkill.

I'll grant that it's an interesting thought, and I have conducted an imaginary argument with this long-dead German on several occasions. I've even looked up pictures of him in order to visualize the scene better. I have to admit that he sported a very impressive mustache. But I will not be deterred from holding on to hope as a force for good. I've imagined telling Nietzsche that I profoundly disagree with him: I don't think hope prolongs our torment, rather that it can end our despair—a torment in itself.

In my mind, I've always won my argument of course, but I was delighted to discover that it appears as though Nietzsche revisited his ideas about hope in later life. He admitted that hope does indeed have a transformative power that can make our lives better. As he wrote in *Thus Spoke Zarathustra*: "do not throw away the hero in your soul! Keep sacred your highest hope!"

It was in 2011 that it became clear to me that my own levels of hope were in need of some serious attention. I was at the Edinburgh Festival in Scotland with a musical I had cowritten about nineteenth-century dentistry and the discovery of anesthetics. It was a comedy (even though it doesn't sound like it). We were at the beginning of our run and we were all sitting bleary-eyed, with the obligatory mild hangovers of those festival days, in the City Cafe, one of my favorite places in Edinburgh. The news suddenly caught my eye. The television was on in the corner, but the sound was turned down, so all we took in were apocalyptic images. London was burning; the full-scale riots on screen looked like civil war. What began as a peaceful protest following the fatal shooting of a young Black man, Mark Duggan, by the police in Tottenham, North London, had exploded and spread across the whole of the U.K.

It was horrible to be away from home at that time, to be worried about friends and neighbors and loved ones, to see pictures of buses on fire, people leaping from burning buildings and businesses destroyed.

For me, it was the last straw. While I had been living my life, in my peripheral vision, almost out of sight, was my mounting fear and despair about racism, climate change, sea levels rising, exploitation of the poor, the growing lists of endangered and extinct species, sex trafficking, child abuse, on and on and on. This stuff had been making me uneasy for so long. What could I—just one person with no power or influence—do about any one of these awful things, let alone all of them? What was the point of donating to WWF or to a homeless shelter when the problems of the world were so huge, insurmountable, and hopeless? How was me wearing bloomers for a living while reciting comedic and disrespectful poetry about the royal family in a nightclub in Soho doing anything to help make the world a better place? I concluded sadly that there was nothing I could do about the terrible mess we were in, and that bloomer wearing and mucking about were all I could offer.

A few days later, on August 18, 2011, I was in the post office. The boy in front of me was talking to the man who worked behind the counter, explaining that he didn't have enough money to pay for his stamp for his driving license application. When I gave him the 50p he needed, he thanked me tearfully. The man at the post office counter said, "That was nice of you," and as I watched the boy walk out, an idea was beginning to form. Without a well-thought-out plan, and with my usual impulsiveness, I decided at that moment to try to do one kind thing for a stranger every single day for a year and to see, as I said to my partner, Gareth, when I arrived home, if "kindness can change the world."

Well, I can now report with confidence that this was, without a doubt, the best 50p I've ever spent. My life and my bruised heart were utterly transformed by this foolhardy endeavor. I practiced kindness every day for those promised 366 days (it covered a leap year). I recognized pretty early on that this would become a lifelong thing: I would never be an "expert," for there would always be more to learn, but it would keep giving me an abundance of joy. It was also, sometimes, a pain in the arse, when it didn't go according to plan or when it resulted in unexpected minor injuries (such as doing my back in when helping someone with an extremely heavy case) or expense (when I offered to pay for someone's shopping without realizing quite how much it would be). But most days it was amazing, and kindness became a part of who I am. So I kept going.

That year changed my life. Seeing that the world wasn't such a bad place reminded me of the importance of hope in dark times. I found that deciding to do something, and then actually doing it, can transform your life. I took action. They were not always successful actions, not always sensible actions, but actions nonetheless. And by taking action, I carved a happy, meaningful, hopeful life.

Having said all of this, I also absolutely acknowledge that it is not always easy to "do something," to recover from disappointments or to stop being scared. All we can do, at any one time, is our best, and I won't ask more of you (or myself) than that. I really do know how difficult life can be. Sometimes I forget to get dressed, spend all day in my pajamas, and then eat chocolate brownies for my dinner. Some days I am grumpy, even when the sky is blue. I have never, in any of the usual contemporary definitions of success—lots of money, possessions, power—been successful. I have suffered, as every human being has in their own ways. I'm a survivor of childhood sexual abuse. I have been poor (like "being a bit hungry and not having much money for food," "the soles are coming off my shoes so I'll glue them on," "I'll sofa-surf for a few months" poor) and have experienced homelessness. I have felt defeated and sad and angry. I've spent all day crying on occasion and other days shouting at the terrible news on the TV in impotent rage.

However, I most definitely have blessings aplenty, and it does help to remember them. I've experienced the privilege of being born in and living in a democratic country with a social welfare system, free healthcare, free education, and clean water. I have never experienced discrimination based on my race, ethnicity, or nationality. I have good friends, a lovely partner, and a family who are loving, supportive, and dependable. I make a living doing what I love. I am an ordinary person who has had an extraordinary journey as I sought out hope in the face of despair. And along the way, I've met some amazing people, uncovered projects all over the world doing incredible things and found an abundance of hope. I finished this journey joyfully, and I truly believe that you will too.

The hope I discovered in myself and in others was not the "cross your fingers behind your back," "thoughts and prayers," "wish upon a star" kind of hope (not that I have anything against any of those things). Instead, this is the sort of hope that gives you strength, that helps you become more resilient because it invites you to take action, however small, to move yourself toward it. This book is an invitation to start your own journey toward hope. You'll discover different treasures, encounter different pitfalls, face different fears than I have perhaps. You'll discover different answers and experience different pleasures on the way, because of course we are each unique, but I'll be keeping you company the whole time.

We're going to begin by looking at ourselves and our individual lives, finding ways to approach hope in our everyday and how we might hang on to it or create it in the most challenging of circumstances. We're going to explore how to find hope with others, through the communities we make or join, and how this can help us to take positive and hope-filled action further. And we're going to look at what all of this might mean for finding hope in the wider world and in our future.

To help us along the way, I've included practical exercises, ideas, and tips, as well as questions you might like to consider. You may find some of them immediately inspiring, while others might help spark your own ideas that you'd prefer to follow. There is no one-size-fits-all approach, so pick and choose whatever suits you. You'll also find lesser-known historical stories of individual triumphs and reminders of times that have been fraught with challenge, when it looked as though things could never get better (yet, lo and behold, they did). And while I quickly discovered that moving toward hope means confronting our fears along the way, I have kept things light-hearted wherever possible. I'm not going to shy away from the global challenges we are facing right here, right now, as well as the regular ones we all experience as part of being human: illness, death, and things just being really tough sometimes. But please don't worry. This is a gentle book. I will be right here alongside you all the way. I promise you're in safe hands.

After that first year of kindness, my work and my life had changed hugely. I began lots of different creative projects with different communities, always with storytelling, kindness, and hope at the heart. I believe that stories are one very powerful way that we make sense of being human, and that stories of kindness, triumph over adversity, courage, action, and connectivity are among those that give us hope. So this book is full of stories, real and imagined, true life and folk tales, stories from history and stories of an imagined future, the stories of where I found hope and how I learned to be hopeful. I believe that active hope increases the chances that our future can be better and our present lives happier. I hope that by sharing these stories I'll prove it to you.

I'd like to return briefly to Emily Dickinson's poem "'Hope' is the thing with feathers," which I quoted at the beginning of this introduction. In the next part of the poem she continues:

> And sweetest – in the Gale – is heard –
> And sore must be the storm –

That could abash the little Bird
That kept so many warm –

I've heard it in the chillest land –
And on the strangest Sea –
Yet – never – in Extremity,
It asked a crumb – of me.

I love this poem. I imagine that little bird, Hope, helping us all to stay warm and comforting us. And yet, even if—as the poem says—she doesn't ask anything of us, I think it's time for us to offer something in return. As we set forth on our journey to find hope, let's make her this promise: we will take action; we will help ourselves, each other, and our world. We will try to have courage, we will help each other to be brave. We will look for silver linings on the cloudiest of days. And I hope we will have lots of fun and find lots of joy along the way. Let's go...

CHAPTER ONE
ordinary days

NURTURING HOPE IN THE EVERYDAY

....

"NORMAL DAY, LET ME BE AWARE
OF THE TREASURE YOU ARE."

—MARY JEAN IRION

ONE MORNING A FEW YEARS ago, I took my dog, Lola, for a walk around the docklands close to where I live. It was cold enough to make miniature clouds of my breath. The trees were fancily dressed in their October best: a rich display of burgundy, mustard, and rust, with the sky a forget-me-not blue. I sat on a bench for a while and watched a flock of geese fly in an arrow over the woods. A man threw a stick for his dog nearby and shouted out, "Oi! Fetch that, Gizmo!" which made me laugh. The man waved at me and I waved back. On the path beside me, written in childlike handwriting with pink chalk, were the words "Hello everyone here" plus a smiley face.

It was an ordinary day. It was also utterly, heart-achingly beautiful. I thought about the world and how many countless other incredible places and inspiring people there are, how much there is all around us to generate awe and wonder. There is a lot to be excited and joyful about, there is plenty of fun to be had, I thought. I was so grateful to be alive in that moment. I felt extremely lucky, and I enjoyed that feeling. I walked home and thought about how important it was to take time to notice all the good stuff.

Of course, it's not always possible or easy for us to find the joy in our "ordinary days." As adults, most of us have many responsibilities and sometimes they can make finding pleasure in the moment a bit of a struggle. We have to work, look after our families, manage our finances, all that humdrum day-to-day stuff, before we even begin to consider the bigger picture of the wider world and all its opportunities and challenges. Our jobs, relationships, all the choices we make as we journey through life can be boring as well as exciting, stressful as well as relaxing.

There's no doubt that it can be hard to maintain hope in the midst of the daily grind: when you're squashed onto a train in rush hour, crushed up against a stranger's armpit, scrolling through pictures of other people on vacation; when you get the fourth gently patronizing rejection in a week for a job you didn't really want anyway; when the bus doesn't stop because the driver didn't see you; when your feet get wet because the roads are full potholes and you can't afford new trainers; when you're not sure where the money you need for this month is going to come from. And we can sometimes criticize ourselves very harshly when we're feeling run-down.

So it's important that we look at how we might navigate the everyday, "ordinary" challenges and make hope a part of our daily lives, before we move on to the bigger trials all humans face—such as anxiety, loss, and grief—and how we create hope there.

What can be really helpful in getting through life's little challenges is to identify the specific things that give *you* a boost of hope. If we can pay attention to what helps us to foster a more resilient and positive attitude in our day-to-day, this can become a kind of bedrock to help to keep us hopeful, whatever comes our way. One thing that really helps me is allowing myself to appreciate the beauty in the world around us at every opportunity.

try this:
EVERYDAY BEAUTY

Make a habit of noticing one beautiful thing every day. This can be as simple as the reflection of streetlights in puddles, an architectural feature of a building you pass frequently, a loved one's smile or laughter, dogs playing in the park. Once you've noticed it, allow yourself a few moments to enjoy it. I find that these short periods of appreciation and reflection make me feel more hopeful about what's good in the world, especially when I feel a bit overwhelmed. If we can focus on the everyday beauty all around us, if only for a short time, it can give us a breath of respite—a moment of pause to allow our minds to take a step back.

A good way to begin thinking about hope in your everyday is simply by spending some dedicated time considering the things that you find inspiring, that cheer you and put a smile on your face. The more aware you are of what brings you joy, the easier it will be to know what to do when you need a bit of a pick-me-up.

If you find it tough to get started, that's okay. I sometimes imagine hope as a single candle in a massive pitch-black cave— it's not going to show us the whole cave, but it will highlight a few glimmers of detail, enough to help ground us and keep fear at bay. We're not looking for any big "solutions" in this chapter: hope can be found in the smallest of things. It could simply be the neighbor who looks after an elderly friend, a warm welcome and a cup of tea in your local community center, or the nettles in your garden covered in caterpillars (because not weeding is a win for both you and nature).

I have listed a few of my hopeful things here, some found closer to home, some farther afield. Yours might be completely different: scientific and technological innovations, people, places, works of art, whatever takes your fancy. I've written down what gives me hope, but also why, because it can make our connection to that thing much stronger and help us figure out what hope looks and feels like to each of us as individuals.

What: The pianos that are left on the concourse at train stations, free for anyone to play.

Why: People have the chance to play and to share their love of music. They give some space and time for strangers to come together and enjoy something beautiful for free.

What: Children planting edible playgrounds in their primary schools.

Why: Kids have the chance to become more connected to nature and will cherish and protect it better than we have done. They will know how to grow their food.

What: The ex-poacher turned wildlife protector I read about in South Africa.

Why: Human beings can have the courage and humility to change their minds and their lives. Other people will support their change, and still more people will see that happen and be encouraged by it.

What: That nobody knows with absolute certainty what the future holds.

Why: It could be wonderful.

try this:
MAKE A HOPE COLLECTION

I found it really useful to gather the things that make me hopeful together in a scrapbook—what I call my hope collection. This way, they can't simply slip away and be forgotten or pushed out by the day-to-day cares we all experience. You may be the kind of person who prefers drawing or taking pictures, doodling, or even making audio recordings. We're all different. I'd recommend putting a notebook in your bag or putting a stack of paper and a pen next to your bed, so you can add to it whenever inspiration strikes. I add to my collection a couple of times a week.

Try not to edit yourself or make harsh judgments about your choices—whatever gives you hope is the right thing, and nobody need see them but you. Your hope collection is there for you whenever you need it, to remind you that there is a lot about which to be hopeful.

As well as focusing on the beautiful, positive things around us—which already give us small glimmers of hope—it can also be really helpful to consider the things we enjoy doing, that can help us relax and recuperate. Even when nothing particularly bad is happening, daily life and responsibilities can slowly overwhelm us and lead to burnout if we don't find ways to manage them. When you lose yourself in an activity you enjoy, you can experience what psychologists call "flow"—becoming completely immersed, energized, and focused. It's the antithesis to constant online multitasking, scrolling, and flitting between social media accounts. This state of "flow" is said to have multiple benefits, including a sense of positivity and courageousness, as well as enabling us to accomplish something worthwhile. This also helps to instill within us the belief that we can make a difference in our lives. And of course, this time taken for ourselves can also help give us the necessary respite we need.

Ben Hogbin is the founder of Discover Wellness and an advanced facilitator of an evidence-based practice called the Wellness Recovery Action Plan. One of the key concepts of WRAP is hope: once you identify and put into practice what makes you feel better in your day-to-day life, you can look forward to the future and "get well, stay well, and go on to meet your life dreams and goals." WRAP empowers individuals with the tools and framework to do this, creating the best possible conditions for hope to grow. Intrigued, I attended one of the WRAP courses that Ben was cofacilitating, wanting to find out more.

The experience encourages people to take the time to get to know themselves and helps get them started through a series of exercises that explore our strengths, our roles and responsibilities, our hobbies and interests. It may sound simple, but many of us in the group realized that we'd never taken time to consider these things properly before.

Ben explained that hope "means different things, to different people, at different times" and told me what it looked like for him: "For me there are three key ingredients: a sense of control in my life, belief in something I value so I have a purpose and a goal, and I need to feel part of a community. When I have those things, I feel I have hope and then I feel well; it gives me a direction in which to travel."

We were asked to think about what hope looks like for us. I realized that for me it's being able to have fun while feeling as though I'm making a tangible contribution to positive change in the world, and making sure that I have time, peace, and quiet when I need it. We also discussed what despair looks like for us and "wellness tools," the things we might use to bring us back to hope from despair should we feel ourselves drifting there. Ben puts it like this: "We already have these things, we just don't label them as wellness tools. They are the things we do to make ourselves feel better when we are feeling down and they underpin everything."

try this:
WELLNESS TOOLBOX

First, we need to identify the simple actions that can make us feel better when we feel down. They might be as straightforward as having a cup of tea, cuddling the cat, making something, or watching a film. Ben recommends they be "simple and safe." These things can also be put into one of three categories: do they distract, relax, or energize you, or is it a combination of these things? For example, listening to music might make you feel happy and energize you, whereas having a bath or yoga session might make you feel happy and relax you. When you become aware that you might be drifting toward a feeling of hopelessness, you can identify what you need—is it to feel more relaxed, distracted, or energized?—and then choose the activity that will best support you in that moment. Finding ways to press pause on a situation or feeling—even for a few minutes—can help ensure you don't spiral into despair. Keep a record of what these things are for you. Revisit them at tricky times—you may write a list or even keep objects or items in a box that will remind you of the things that keep you well when you need them.

During Ben's course, we also discussed how much pressure we can sometimes put on ourselves to finish our to-do lists and to get everything sorted all at once. This doesn't leave much oxygen for that little flame of hope to keep on burning.

So, to avoid that feeling of overwhelm, Ben spoke about the

importance of setting yourself little goals and focusing on achievable tasks. Breaking down the big goal—or the next day or week—into smaller steps can help you get things done and bring a focus to what otherwise might feel too enormous for one person to deal with.

Ben used as his example U.S. Navy Admiral William H. McRaven, who champions the importance of simple things, such as making your bed every morning. By doing so, he says that you will experience the pride of having completed that first task of the day and that this achievement will encourage you to do another (and another, and another...). And it will help you see that seemingly insignificant things do matter. Since then, I have made my bed every day, and it works. At the very least, as the admiral says, "If by chance you have a miserable day you will come home to a bed that is made."

Considering this exercise for myself, I'd been thinking for a while that I'd love to do a very long walk, a sort of secular pilgrimage. However, I realized that I'd been putting it off because there was always something that felt more important on my to-do list, like a job application, and the thought of organizing and preparing for a long-distance walk on top of all that was overwhelming. I doubted I could ever achieve it. But I started walking anyway, just short daily walks, no matter what else the week brought. Sometimes I could only manage fifteen minutes, but by doing even that, I experienced a real sense of pride. Each walk constitutes a few small steps toward my bigger dream of setting off on a walk of a thousand miles and increases my hope that one day I will achieve it.

Small actions really can make a difference when we feel that the daily grind is becoming too much for us. I often feel despair that I'll never have enough time to do all the things that I feel I should do, and at times like this, it's important to find small ways of looking after ourselves to help us deal with the everyday challenges we face. Charlotte Wiseman, a positive psychologist who studies what makes life meaningful, says that even breathing deeply for a few seconds can work wonders and help give us the space we need.

Charlotte began studying applied positive psychology after experiencing burnout herself. Following a long battle with eating disorders, she threw herself into her work and stopped making time for other aspects of her life, and after a particularly intense period, her mental health took a sharp decline, leaving her exhausted and hopeless. It was through the recovery process that she slowly discovered how to look after herself. Now her expertise includes teaching people how to manage their daily stress and challenges, helping them to live in fulfilling and satisfying ways.

She and I arranged to meet in a café by the river in South London and decided to walk and people-watch, like twenty-first-century flaneurs out on a stroll. It was the "magic hour," the violet light of dusk spilling across the river at its most beautiful. On our wanderings, we came across a dapper street poet selling his handwritten verses on colorful pieces of paper on a blanket on the pavement, then a mustachioed busker whose battered trombone blew out fire with every note. As we walked, we began to talk about the connection between hope and self-care, and some of the simple acts you can incorporate into your daily routine that can make a world of difference.

One of the things Charlotte has found has a positive effect on her well-being and productivity is taking time out throughout the day:

We need to take breaks every 90 to 120 minutes in order to maintain focus and cognitive performance, to ensure our nervous systems can recalibrate so we can think rationally and not get overwhelmed, and to re-energize and refuel our minds. I find that three five- to ten-minute breaks a day is a minimum for me to be productive, positive, and well.

Charlotte also explained that so often we think about what we haven't done—our perceived weaknesses or failings—rather than focusing on what we *have* achieved. Charlotte suggested that if we can acknowledge our strengths, accomplishments, or what makes us unique, this will inevitably help us to feel stronger and more hopeful about what we're able to deal with or achieve.

One of the most powerful tools I ever discovered was recognizing the "strengths" I have shown in a day. Like most people, I was very good at thinking about what I had not done well, what I "should" do more of, what I was not good at. I started then, and continue now, to finish each day identifying what character strengths I have used and noticing how they have helped me.

try this:
MY STRENGTHS

This is an exercise that I find so helpful and comforting, inspired by the conversation I had with Charlotte.

At the end of each day, think of one thing that you achieved. You don't even have to feel as if you did it very well. On a good day, it might be something like "I managed to swim ten laps in the pool." On a day that's felt much harder, it might be: "I managed to get out of bed."

Now think of something positive that doing this thing revealed about you. For example, with the swimming it could be "I am strong, energetic, and really committed to staying healthy." Or on the day when you didn't feel you'd be able to do much more than lift the bedcover, you might think, "I did get up and got on with things. I was brave and strong because it would have been so much easier to stay in bed." If you do this exercise every day, you will be paying attention to those little things that so often go unacknowledged, all those everyday triumphs and strengths that we don't take the time to congratulate ourselves for. It's a gentle way of loving and taking care of yourself. For me, it specifically helps with a sense of hope because every day I realize that I have achieved something. And in turn, this makes me feel hopeful that in the future I will be able to cope with what comes my way, as I have done many times before.

There's no doubt that making the time for these daily exercises can help bring us moments of calm and a renewed sense of achievement, creating more fertile ground for hope. However, when we're really overwhelmed, "one foot in front of the other" can feel more than enough. If you're feeling this way, try to step back from taking the weight of the world upon yourself and focus on being truly gentle with your mind and body as you get through the tasks and obligations of this day, and then the next. We'll come back to this in chapter three as we consider how we find hope on "rainy days."

Remembering to treat ourselves—as well as others—with patience and kindness reminds me of the Egyptian poet Mostafa Ibrahim, who wrote these beautiful words:

May you never be the reason why someone who loved to sing doesn't sing anymore. Or why someone who dressed so differently now wears standard clothing. Or why someone who always spoke their dreams so wildly is now silent about them.

I think that this "someone" can sometimes be us, that we can do this damage to ourselves. With negative self-talk about our inadequacies or perceived shortfalls, we can overlook what makes us unique, diminishing our courage and weakening that flickering flame.

If your present situation is making you feel this way, I'd love to invite you to try something I've found incredibly helpful as a way of countering my inner critic. I was introduced to this exercise in an improvisation course ran by an inspirational teacher called Logan Murray. He set us this task—"My Wonderful Life So Far"—as a way of helping us to generate comedic material. However, I've used it since when leading creative workshops to encourage people to tell the stories of their lives in a positive way, to focus on their rich experience.

try this:
MY WONDERFUL LIFE SO FAR

For this exercise, you can write things down or record yourself speaking, whichever you prefer. The idea is to tell the story of your life, focusing on the positives—all the highlights—especially if you think your life is boring, or ordinary, or that you haven't done much to speak of. Start with your birth and go all the way up to today. Make sure you include everything that you enjoyed or of which you feel proud. These can be big things like passing your driving test or small things like enjoying your best friend's wedding. Give as much detail as possible: that unplanned "perfect" day, the night you laughed with friends until you cried, the relationships that have brought you such joy, the person you helped. If you drift into negativity, pause, refocus on the positive, and carry on. Remind yourself that the purpose of this exercise is to express only the good stuff.

When you're done, listen or read it back, and enjoy it. Linger on all the amazing things you've done and experienced. Consider how far you've come, and how far you can still go. Focusing on your achievements will bolster your hope for your future, even if your present isn't quite what you want it to be. You'll probably feel pretty good too, as when we focus on happy memories our brains produce serotonin, so we get a rush of pleasure.

If you get a chance to do this with a friend, even better. You can take turns and gently steer each other back to positive stories if you veer off course. One of my friends admitted that she did feel much more positive after trying this with me.

Another really useful approach to getting to a place of increased hopefulness in your day-to-day is practicing "on the bright side" thinking. At the Greater Good Science Center of the University of Berkeley, they study the psychology, sociology, and neuroscience of well-being. The experts there have devised a practice called Finding Silver Linings, which encourages us to find the best in the bad.

try this:
SILVER LININGS

List five things that make you feel that your life is worth-while or enjoyable. This will help you to shift yourself into a positive frame of mind.

Once you've done this, write about a recent time when things didn't go your way, when you got frustrated, irritated, or upset.

Then list three things that might help you to see the bright side of this situation.

For example: you broke your favorite cup this morning.

1. You have plenty of other cups.
2. You didn't hurt yourself when you broke it, so there was no real harm done.
3. In a few weeks' time, you probably won't even remember the cup.

They recommend that you do this every day for three weeks. The poet Maggie Smith tried this exercise and spoke about her experience on the *Science of Happiness* podcast. She said that although it was sometimes "just too soon or too painful to see the bright side of something," she knew that she could "return to it later, or leave it be." For her the practice "did make me feel more hopeful, as it allows for the possibility of change."

Another type of bright-side thinking is to positively reframe a negative experience. For example, it's fair to say that the inventor Thomas Edison failed a few times before he successfully created his lightbulb. But what Edison said about this was "I have not failed. I've just found 10,000 ways that won't work."

In our own lives too, we are the tellers of the story of ourselves. Like Edison, we can choose to reframe our experiences in a more positive way, helping to remove the sting from potentially difficult memories and experiences. This doesn't mean denying anything; rather, it means not letting the painful situation have all the power, especially if it's taking away pleasure or impetus in your present or hope for your future.

In my own life, my dad broke contact completely with my sister and me when I was only three years old. He never tried to get back in touch. For a long time, I told myself it was my fault for somehow not being "enough" for him. Later I told myself that despite my dad's absence, my sister and I had thrived and turned to each other for support and guidance. I changed the story from one of heartbroken rejection to one of our triumph over adversity (and I forgave my dad too).

I like to imagine that each of the 10,000 times that Edison's lightbulb didn't turn on, he said something like "I'm so glad that didn't work because I've got a better idea." He hoped it would work, and he took action to make that happen. My own lightbulb moment was realizing when I read this story that it isn't just about reframing our stories in a more positive light; we also need to practice active hope. To realize our dreams, we need to act on them.

try this:
TIME TRAVEL FOR OPTIMISTS

I know it sometimes takes strength to imagine something better for yourself, but once you've imagined it, you can begin to work out how to get there from where you are. It's all about breaking it down.

1. Visualize what you'd like your future to look like. Take your time. Fill in as many details as you like. Enjoy yourself imagining.

2. Verbalize your desires by expressing them out loud. These are your "magic words," so make them positive. For example, if you want to be healthier, you could say "I want to eat healthier and get more exercise" rather than "I don't want to feel bad about my body and health." Using positive words will help you focus on the solution rather than the problem.

3. Decide on one small action for the next week that will begin to carry you forward in your imagined

direction. It could be doing research to find the information you need to take that next steps, identifying and calling a friend or acquaintance who might be able to help you, or signing up for a course to get the skills you need. Anything that serves your hope for your future, whatever that looks like to you. I always feel a real sense of achievement whenever I do this, as I know I have made a start, however small.

Of all the advice I have ever been given as a way of feeling stronger, happier, and more hopeful in day-to-day "ordinary" life, the very best was from Doris, ninety-four years young. When I met her, she had "all sorts of aches and pains," and she had lost her beloved husband and her son. She told me she sang every day, and that every single night she counted her blessings, reminding herself of all the reasons she had to be hopeful that tomorrow would be a good day. Much has been said and written about gratitude for what we already have, and since chatting with Doris about how powerful it is, I can only agree.

I invite you to try this with me. Each evening, I bring the day to a close by focusing on one thing I feel thankful for about that day: it could be a bit of sunshine, a bird at my window, something that made me laugh. I follow this up by thinking about all the things I'm grateful for—my friends, family, home, work—which we can so easily take for granted. I do this every single night just before bed, so that even after a humdrum, ordinary day I go to sleep feeling more hopeful about tomorrow, having brought to mind the many ways in which I am blessed in my everyday life.

CHAPTER TWO
our younger selves

RECAPTURING THE OPTIMISM OF CHILDHOOD

....

"EVEN IN THE GRIMMEST OF SITUATIONS
WITHOUT TOO MUCH ENCOURAGEMENT,
CHILDREN LOVE TO PLAY,
TO INVENT STORIES."

—CLOWNS WITHOUT BORDERS UK

I N 2015, I WAS IN Birmingham, delivering a workshop with primary-school kids about heroes. We talked about who their heroes were—famous or otherwise—and why. We talked about their favorite superheroes and what they loved about them. Then we moved on to envisaging the best world that we could possibly imagine. The kids called out ideas including "no bullies," "no sad people," and "everyone has food." Then they created their own superheroes who would help make it happen. They came up with some great examples, including the Ninja of Niceness—a superhero who used their power of kindness to make everyone smile. There was also the Loud Lord of Laughter, whose superpower was cheering up sick kids in hospital with very silly jokes and impressions, and Terror Tidy, a hero who was really fast at clearing up mess and got rid of all the litter. They improvised plays showing how these superheroes defeated bullies, sadness, and rubbish. They had absolutely no doubt that the skills they already had could sort out the problems in the world. One little girl said to me, "We should actually do this, miss, don't you think? We could make some masks and costumes and we could do it. In real life or just start off in a play." It was a hilarious, hopeful, fun day.

I've taught and worked with children a lot over the last ten years, delivering storytelling, creative workshops and developing children's theater shows. One of the things that strikes me every time I'm around kids is how hopeful they seem almost all of the time. In my experience if you ask a class of children "Shall we try this?" or "Do you think this is a good idea?" the answer nine times out of ten is an extremely loud "Yes!" followed by a huge amount of energy and enthusiasm for doing that thing as soon as possible. If you ask them how they think it will go, the responses are "Amazing," "It'll be brilliant," and "Awesome."

I began thinking about whether there had been any academic or scientific studies into how and why so many children seem to have a more positive attitude than adults. I also wondered if there was anything we could learn about hope from their approach to life. Is there a way for us to reach back into our own childhoods for some inspiration or insight into how we saw the world back then?

As I looked into the possibilities, I came across the work of Janet J. Boseovski, an associate professor of psychology at the University of North Carolina. She's interested in what she describes as children's "rose-tinted glasses"—otherwise known as their "positivity bias." In her work she describes this as "a tendency to focus on positive actions or selectively process information that promotes positive judgments about the self, others, or even animals and objects." Psychologists aren't yet sure *why* so many kids have this positivity bias, but Boseovski says it's "likely due in part to the positive social experiences that most children are lucky enough to have early in life." If we are fortunate as children, we're protected from dangers and discomfort, praised often, and encouraged to find pleasure and enjoyment in our lives.

Her research included investigating why young children are "strikingly less cautious when making character judgments"—in other words, why they expect people to be nice. With her colleagues, she discovered that "three- to six-year-olds only need to see one positive behavior to judge a story character as nice, but several negative behaviors to judge a character as mean."

Boseovski's studies revealed that the "positivity bias" emerges in children as young as three years old, reaches its peak in middle childhood (usually defined as ages six to twelve), and weakens as children get older and through life experience are exposed to harsher realities. And so when communicating difficult things such as critical feedback or bad news to children, she recommends that it should be done in a loving way, with encouragement and support to keep that positivity bolstered. I imagine this encouragement as a cheerleader standing by our sides saying, "Come on, you can do it! Don't give up!"

By the time we reach adulthood, having had to deal with the many knocks life can bring, we may find our positivity bias has faded away. Reading Boseovski's research made me think that we need to learn to be our own cheerleaders. We need to gently accept that the world isn't perfect—and neither are we—but find a positive aspect to focus on. If we can learn to see disappointment, criticism, even suffering, as a chance to learn and grow rather than as devastating and defeating, it will give us a much better chance of remaining hopeful. Perhaps we'll never regain the rose-tinted glasses of early childhood, but we can be more positive and forward-looking nonetheless.

try this:
SMALL STEPS

Every day presents a different set of challenges, and a hopeful attitude can turn a negative experience around.

The next time something feels like it has gone wrong, try asking yourself: What could you enjoy learning from that experience? How would you hope to improve, and what do you need to do to make that happen? This is always possible, no matter how challenging the experience has been. To give you an example: I started a fantastic theater job a few years ago. But one week after we began rehearsals, the director called me to tell me it wasn't working and she would have to replace me. I was absolutely devastated and it took me a while to work out what I could possibly learn from this awful and humiliating experience.

I realized that in my heart of hearts I knew I wasn't right for the job when I got it and that I should have listened to myself and turned it down, which would have saved me a lot of heartache and worry. I also learned from that time how to take care of myself when things didn't go my way and what I needed to recover my happiness and hopefulness. I learned to focus on my strengths and to bravely face the areas in which I needed to improve.

If you are feeling low or defeated by what you perceive as a failure, restore your positivity by remembering what you are really good at while also committing to working on your weaknesses, just a little, one day at a time.

As I wondered what else we might recreate or learn from our childhood in terms of a more hopeful outlook, I began to think about some of the things that children experience more than adults. The very first thing that sprang to mind was that kids are encouraged to believe in magic. While I absolutely love what this brings to children's lives, I don't think making a wish as we blow out a birthday candle will be of much practical help when it comes to bolstering our hope as grown-ups. It's a passive approach that doesn't encourage us to act, but to wait for a miracle.

Thinking about magic, however, did lead me to another big feature in children's lives: stories. Stories are a great example of true "magic words." The right words, told in the right order, can transform a reader or listener from happy to sad, from bored to entertained, from despairing to hopeful. I see the power of this every day as a storyteller. So perhaps there is something in the magic of storytelling that as adults we can use to become more hopeful.

As kids, we almost always hear stories with happy endings, where hard work and kindness are rewarded, fears and enemies defeated or better still turned into friends. Even stories that are emotionally complex and dark—like one of my childhood favorites, *Watership Down*, which has a lot of sadness and conflict thrown in—still culminate in a happy ending. When faced by monsters, floods, evil spirits, ravenous beasts, or angry teachers, as children we learn that if we act in hope we will prevail.

However, as adults we have learned that the world can be unfair and unjust, that good behavior isn't always rewarded, and that happy endings certainly aren't guaranteed. Once we know the world doesn't always work in that fairy-tale way, how can those kinds of stories serve us?

Perhaps as adults they can't help us in quite the same way, but I do think we can come to see that while "happily ever after" isn't always the way things work out, neither is "everything always goes wrong." If we wallow only in bleak, hopeless, doom-laden narratives (popular culture for adults is awash with those!), this too is unrealistic. What we can learn from children's stories and the pleasure they bring is the importance of making time for positive, hopeful stories too. Stories that inspire us, remind us that there are good people doing wonderful things out there. If we're feeling down, sometimes a happy ending, a story of redemption or of justice winning the day can be just what we need to give us a positive boost and motivate us to take hopeful action ourselves.

try this:
HAPPY ENDINGS

Think about what your most cherished story was as a child, whether it was a film, TV show, game, or book. What was it you loved about this story? If you read or watch it again now, does it give you the same feelings it did then? It's interesting to think about the messages these stories delivered to us as impressionable kids and to remind ourselves of what encouraged or entertained us.

Now think about the stories you enjoy as an adult.

How do they differ from the ones you enjoyed as a child? What are the messages of the stories you absorb today and how do they make you feel? Do they encourage you or inspire you? Or do they communicate a negative or fearful message? If the latter, consider what effect that might be having on your outlook.

Two further tools that children have at their fingertips, but which are sometimes set aside as we reach adulthood, are our imaginations and ability to play. Anyone who has watched kids play can see the enormous joy they experience as they act out and become absorbed in the miniature world they have conjured with their imaginations, experiencing that sense of "flow" we discussed earlier.

Last year, I was back in schools doing some more storytelling with classes of eight-year-old children, this time on the theme of the future. The kids were very hopeful about the future, largely because of the scientific and technological inventions and innovations they imagined. For example, they said they'd like to invent a giant machine to suck all the plastic out of the ocean and "to make it into food for animals."

They said they wanted to grow giant trees overnight that would "suck up the pollution quickly." They said they would invent cars that "told you jokes and ran on solar panels"; they would make sure that "there would be no hungry kids anywhere" and that "homeless people and animals could live in big, nice houses with water slides." These kids had strong ideas about social and climate justice. They were quick, brave, and playful with their inventions. They weren't afraid to think big and to imagine the incredible.

They imagined fun things for their futures too, like jet packs, robot butlers, guns that shoot marshmallows into your mouth, edible rainbows made of sherbet, and talking dogs. In other words, they imagined things many of us probably secretly want but have stopped allowing ourselves to hope for.

Although a lot of effort is needed to turn an idea—like a robot butler—into a reality, the hard work couldn't even begin without someone having the courage to imagine it first. Imagination gives us something to aim for. Many great inventions have emerged from the creative visions of science fiction, for example. But as adults, we can forget to let our imaginations run riot as we did when we were young. We need to take a lesson from the audacious inventiveness of children and recognize how invaluable such creativity is: an incredible tool for problem solving and for imagining new ways of being or doing things, a way of creating a hopeful vision for our futures. Einstein once wrote, "Imagination is more important than knowledge. For knowledge is limited, whereas imagination embraces the entire world, stimulating progress, giving birth to evolution."

The history of aviation is a good example of this. For millennia, humans had fantasies of flight. Several centuries BC, the Chinese were flying probably the first human-made aircraft: kites. In the fifteenth century, Leonardo da Vinci drew beautiful but scientifically unrealistic flying machines that he never attempted to construct. One of my favorite stories of early attempts at flight is from 1507, when John Damian strapped on wings covered in chicken feathers, jumped from the walls of Stirling Castle in Scotland, tumbled to the ground, and broke his thigh, blaming his failure on the fact that he'd not used eagle feathers.

Still, despite all the failures and setbacks, and the accepted "knowledge" that humans would never be able to take to the skies, a brave few continued to try, driven by their imaginations. Over the next few centuries, these visionaries slowly made progress, creating a variety of machines and structures powered by hydrogen, wood fire, coal, carrying a variety of passengers including chickens, sheep, scientists, and aristocratic gentlemen, until finally these wild imaginings led us to where we are now: our skies zigzagged with airplanes that allow us to see the wonders of our world. For me, this journey from kites to Concord proves that imagination and invention go hand-in-hand with hope, enabling us to continue to strive forward.

try this:
MY IMAGINARIUM

Imagine something that you would like more of for yourself in the future—it could be more money, more security, a bigger home, a better job, more love, more friends. Use your imagination to vividly envisage what that would look like, build in details, and make it rich. Whatever we hope to create or achieve, we must first imagine it. Once the image is clear in your mind, you can begin to take tiny steps toward making it a reality. Having a clear image of what we want can give us the hope that it is possible to achieve.

There's a really strong intersection between how hope interacts with imagination and how it also interacts with play, which I was lucky enough to explore in a conversation with Marion Duggan. Marion is a former board member of a charity called Clowns Without Borders UK, with whom she also volunteered as a performer. In 2017, this organization went to the mud-filled camps of Northern Greece to play with and perform for the refugee children living there. She told me that "even in the hardest circumstances...the kids find ways to play, in puddles of rain or with old tent poles...I felt sad when I witnessed that, but it was their reality." She went on to tell me that the young people in the camps gave her "the capacity to find hope in difficult situations because of their example: they always try to play and to find joy."

Incredibly, it was children who came up with the idea behind Clowns Without Borders. In 1993, a group of children in Barcelona raised funds to send the clown who entertained them, Tortell

Poltrona, to camps in Croatia. Their refugee pen pals over there had told them that "we miss laughter." This was their solution. The first show attracted audiences of over four thousand children and Poltrona founded Clowns Without Borders in response, helping to show displaced people across the world that others care.

Speaking with Marion made me think back to the idea of children's "positivity bias." Clearly the children in this camp weren't in ideal conditions for ensuring the positive social experiences many children enjoy, but they were still able to find happiness in play— their very real "superpower."

try this:
GAME NIGHT

Think about what you loved to play as a child, whether that's hide-and-seek, chess, or cricket. Rediscover the joy to be found in a simple game and have a games night with friends or family. Give yourself a break from whatever is troubling you, and just focus on one evening of fun and play. Taking the time to do just that is in itself a hopeful act.

As adults trying to seek out hope, we should embrace this knowledge and look out for any opportunity for games, fun, and festivity. According to the Imperial War Museum, during the First World War, the German and British troops met in no-man's-land to exchange gifts, take photographs, and play some impromptu games of soccer, finding a moment of pleasure in the bleakest of circumstances. At the very least, playfulness will take your mind off your troubles for a short while. At best, it can help you see that tomorrow really could be a better day. When you realize you're able to find joy in the moment, there is suddenly hope that there will be many more occasions like this in the future. Remember, the very real magic of a child's playful imagination can transform even muddy fields into a wonderland for a time. Joy and laughter can help us to survive.

try this:
LAUGHTER IS THE BEST MEDICINE

Find something that makes you smile or laugh. Allow yourself to enjoy funny YouTube videos or watch comedy. Sharing laughter with friends gives us a lovely endorphin rush—a natural feel-good buzz that has been proven to bring feelings of calm and pleasure. Laughing is a powerful tool for helping you to be hopeful, letting you know that you will be able to find joy in the future, as you have done today.

If laughter feels too far out of reach, see if you can manage a smile—the simple act of smiling can make you happy as it releases hormones such as dopamine (the "happiness hormone") and serotonin (which can reduce stress). And it has been shown to work even if you don't feel especially happy, in a "fake it till you make it" way.

If you can't quite manage either yet, that's okay too. Sometimes it is just too difficult. But keep yourself open to those bright moments when something does raise a smile or a chuckle, as this really can change your outlook on the future.

As a child, I used to have huge amounts of fun with my grandparents and my sister making up daft limericks around the dinner table. I came to learn later that my grandparents didn't have an easy life, experiencing both extreme poverty and loss. This made me realize that they were both natural optimists, always on the lookout for laughter.

When we're young, witnessing how our parents or caregivers respond to challenges can have a lasting impact on us, shaping how we approach problems later in life. I think it's because of my grandparents that I am so intent on finding hope in any situation. Remembering those positive childhood memories always gives me a boost. Sometimes looking back at the positive moments from our own childhoods can help us find reasons to be hopeful.

Yet there's no doubt that negative memories from our childhoods also have a lasting impact on our relationship with hope.

Often our fears and anxieties have their roots in a bad experience from when we were young. Nevertheless, we can still find ways to overcome them through active hope—identifying what it is you hope to achieve and working out practical steps you can take to make that hope a reality.

My mum nearly drowned on a holiday in Cornwall when she was ten. She vividly recalls even now, over sixty years later, clambering over the rocks with her brother when she was hit by a big wave and pulled under. Ever since, my mum was understandably terrified of deep water and my sisters and I thought she always would be.

Then, to our surprise, we realized we had underestimated her: at the age of fifty-nine, she learned to swim. Despite her vivid childhood memories and the fact that she remained very frightened, she stuck with it. She realized that she would love to be able to swim; she hoped that she would be able to swim; *and* she saw that all of this would require some actionable steps on her part, so she took lessons. And she did it. You are never too old for active hope; you are never too old to change something you learned in childhood that is unhelpful to you right now; you are never too old to be an excellent example for someone else.

All my life, knowing Mum's story and seeing her avoid swimming had also made me afraid of putting my head under. I had developed my mum's fear from her example, and while I did swim a little, I decided that I wouldn't ever be any good at it and that it was my mum's fault. But once I saw her determination, I realized it was a bit unfair for me to blame my fears on her and was inspired to get into swimming too.

try this:
A TALE OF DERRING-DO

Think back to a time in your childhood when an adult in your life did something that seemed brave or daring to you. Write or record this story as a rousing example of hope in action from your life history. It doesn't have to be anything extreme like "she fought off a shark with her bare hands"—it could be as simple as overcoming a fear or trying to change something in their community.

Share the story with a friend or relative who doesn't know it. There is great power, pride, and pleasure to be had from sharing such tales of derring-do. Stories of real, ordinary people—particularly if they're people we know—doing brave, extraordinary things encourage us to dare to hope that we might be able to be brave and extraordinary too.

We all have, in our different ways, challenging, difficult, or painful memories to process from our childhoods, as well as inspiring, funny, and treasured experiences too. There is so much to be learned from the way children approach the world that can stir hope within us. While we're unlikely to be able to fully restore the positivity bias of our earliest years, we *can* make time for happy endings and uplifting stories. We can embrace play and laughter and let our imaginations run wild. We can dare to dream. We can turn what we see in our mind's eye into reality and believe this to be possible. And if we can carry with us some of the mighty tools and skills we learned in childhood and see in the children around us today, hope begins to grow.

CHAPTER THREE
hard times

FINDING HOPE ON THE RAINIEST OF DAYS

....

"IT IS ONLY IN SORROW BAD WEATHER
MASTERS US; IN JOY WE FACE THE
STORM AND DEFY IT."

—AMELIA BARR

I N HER BRILLIANT TEDx TALK, storyteller Vanessa Woolf retells one of her favorite fairy tales, Hans Christian Andersen's "The Snow Queen." In the story, a demon creates a magic mirror with a terrible power: anyone who gazes into its reflection loses the ability to feel joy. It made "everything good and beautiful that was reflected in it shrink to almost nothing, while all that was worthless and bad looked still larger and worse." The demon loves the mirror so much that he decides to take it up to heaven, to show it to the angels. As he flies upward to deliver his mischief, the mirror begins to shake and tremble, and then it breaks into a million pieces that rain down on the earth. This is a disaster: the shards fall into people's eyes, and suddenly they can only see the ugly, boring, and cruel things around them. Some pieces lodge into people's hearts, making them cold and callous. In the story a little boy, Kay, is changed by one of the shards, becoming cruel, and is whisked away from home by the Snow Queen. She takes him far away to her castle, where he soon forgets everything good that he had in his life. Kay's friend Gerda sets out to look for him, with great dedication and determination. She never loses hope, even when her journey is arduous, and when she eventually finds Kay, the warmth of her love thaws his frozen heart, and her tears wash the grain of glass from his eye. He can experience wonder and see beauty once more. Hope is returned to him.

I love this story. It reminds us how easily we adults can slip into only seeing the "ugly, boring, and cruel" around us and how our hope gets eroded, our energy depleted, and our happiness diminished. This really is how life can feel when we're experiencing difficult times. But it also reminds us, as Vanessa went on to discuss, how important it is still to be able to find the "wonder and beauty" during these hardest of days and how we can help ourselves and each other to discover it. One of the toughest things to experience is the loss of a loved one—and we'll be exploring that together in the next chapter. What I want to consider right now is how we stay hopeful through the many other tough challenges life can send our way. Perhaps your daily grind has taken a serious toll, or work stress or financial worries have escalated, or maybe you've had to live through a frightening experience. How then, in the hardest of circumstances, can we keep in view the many miraculous things that fill our world and can help us hold on to hope?

I was in the pub one evening chatting with a friend about maintaining hope in hard times, and she told me an extraordinary story about her pal Tom Hart Dyke. Tom is a gardener whose passion for botany led to him being kidnapped and held hostage for nine months. He told me the full story a few days later.

Tom's beloved grandmother introduced him to gardening when he was three years old: "Here's a packet of carrot seeds and a trowel, Tom. Get your hands dirty." Tom and his granny shared a passion for orchids and as he grew up, he yearned to see tropical varieties in the wild and to "find one to name after Granny." With some small grants and his savings, he managed a few wondrous orchid-hunting trips abroad, during which Tom met mountaineer Paul Winder. Paul told him about the beautiful tropical forests of the Darién Gap on the border between Panama and Colombia. The two set out in March 2000, paying no heed to the warnings of the extreme dangers of that region. Tom described himself and Paul as "idiots" for doing so, but there was also a beautifully reckless optimism about what they did: if everybody heeded warnings, nothing would be achieved.

Nevertheless, Tom explained that soon "we were kidnapped and thrown onto our knees, hands behind our backs, big M16 rifles stuck to our heads." During the time they were held in captivity, they feared for their lives every single day. Their captors forced Tom and Paul to write letters to their families demanding $5 million each for their safe return. The letters never reached their families, and the two men spent the next few months wandering in the jungle with their captors from one makeshift camp to another, not knowing which moment might be their last.

I asked Tom how he endured such an extreme situation. He replied, "I'm not recommending the experience, but after being kidnapped we saw the best orchids ever. It was the orchids that kept me going." Despite their situation, Tom was able to continue searching for and collecting the plants, and in the early days, his captors even helped him. When they stayed in one place for a while, Tom "built gardens around the camp with the orchids as a way of expressing myself and showing them who I was, that I was not a drug runner or CIA agent as they thought."

Eventually they arrived at a place that was too low in altitude for orchids, and Tom told me that was when the hopelessness of his situation started to set in, leading his mindset to shift: "We will die because the money won't come; they'll shoot us, dig a few holes, and bury us. That's what we thought would happen at the end."

Tom knew he had to find something else to occupy his mind, a focus away from their terrible predicament. "I began to plan a garden," he told me. "In my head I could fantasize about how the garden was going to be, so that gave me my real mental strength. Every morning when I woke up, or at night when I was thinking 'I'm going to die,' instead I thought, 'All right, let's have a look at this garden a bit more.'"

His captors were initially baffled and then infuriated by his passion for plants. "My love for orchids drove them nuts in the end," Tom explained, and he and Paul were eventually released just outside Panama, with all their money, possessions, and passports handed back to them. They arrived back on British soil on December 21, 2000, "a year and a bit later than I said I would."

I was enthralled by Tom's story and the ways he'd found to ward off despair. Okay, it's not every day you find yourself held at gunpoint in a tropical jungle, but there are so many lessons to be learned from his experience. In the midst of utter hopelessness and terror, he focused on what he loved, sought out the beauty around him, and gave himself a project on which to concentrate. It seems to me that his love and passion for the natural world got him through the darkest of all imaginable times. Even on the day when a guard said to Tom and Paul, "You've got five hours before we blow your heads off," Tom responded by scribbling further plans for a very special garden in his diary, plans which came to fruition when he planted the World Garden at his family home in Lullingstone Castle in the English countryside. It opened to the public in March 2005.

try this:
FINDING HOPE IN NATURE

If you find yourself having a dark and difficult day, take a moment to appreciate nature. It could be a long walk in the woods or five minutes admiring a flower or a bird singing.

Nature can remind us of resilience, of the wealth and richness that we are surrounded by, and also that things come in cycles: after every winter comes spring. Nothing stays the same forever, so that in the darkness of winter when snow lies thickly on the ground, we can say with absolute certainty, "This too will pass." In the midst of suffering, the reminder of that simple fact can be a great source of hope.

Tom's story is an extreme one, but many of us will undoubtedly have experienced hardships, fears, and uncertainties of our own. Even if there isn't one particularly awful thing that's making life tough, sometimes it can feel hard to keep on going. When I need a pick-me-up to inspire me, I return to one of my favorite poems, "The Summer Day" by Mary Oliver. So when my friend Cat told me she was feeling down, I read her an excerpt, thinking it might help. I find Mary Oliver's words incredibly energizing—they make me feel like walking from London to the Highlands in my bare feet, enrolling in an opera-singing course, or bungee jumping off Niagara Falls. This poem never fails to spur me on, so I hoped that it would work for Cat too.

However, Cat said she found it a little intimidating—that all she could manage to do was get up, go to work, come home, and eat dinner. Nothing dramatic had occurred, but she felt wrung out by what she described as the "daily grind." The quote made her feel that she had to do something amazing, but she didn't think she was capable of that. She also told me that she prefers to be pessimistic because "then I can't be disappointed when it goes wrong, because it usually *does* go wrong." She admitted that often she didn't try things, even if she wanted to, because she felt sure they wouldn't work out.

I thought about this for a long time. Cat is funny, she has a great job that she is good at, she has a nice home and partner, and she has loads of accomplishments. However, she told me that she does tend to focus on the negatives and is sometimes sad because of that. I can see how pessimism could protect you from the pain of disappointment, but if hopelessness stops us from even trying, we miss out on a potentially enjoyable experience, as well as on the possibility of success. If we don't take action to make even small changes in our lives or our world, and we can never see the bright side, this negativity can understandably become overwhelming and take a toll on our mental health.

try this:
SET A GOAL

If you're feeling hopeless and overwhelmed by a seemingly insurmountable problem, finding a purpose can help you by providing another focus. Think of something you've always wanted to do—it doesn't have to be something epic like climbing Everest, and it doesn't have to cost much/any money. It could be finishing that half-read book or running a 5K, filling your balcony with herbs or putting up some beautiful shelving. Choose something that excites or interests you, something that you can look forward to doing.

Focus on how you're going to get started. Break it down step-by-step and set aside periods of time to focus on it, so you can clearly see how you're going to achieve your goal. Purpose can help us be hopeful as it shows us how capable we are of doing something worthwhile that brings us a sense of achievement or joy. You may then feel more able to tackle thornier issues once it's clear that you're capable of taking action that makes a difference and gets results.

My conversation with Cat made me wonder how common a pessimistic attitude is in adults. I came across the work of Dr. Rick Hanson, a neuropsychologist who has studied his own "negativity" bias. He realized that he was expecting the worst and experiencing despair, even when nice things were actually happening. It was hard for him to enjoy positive experiences in the moment and very difficult to feel hopeful about the future. He wondered why this was and if there was anything he could do about it.

Dr. Hanson's fascinating work explores why humans might

be prone to pessimism: in part, it's the way our human minds have evolved over millions of years. I find it easiest to understand as a story about our ancestors, in particular a woman living on earth thousands of years ago, whom I've called Adede.

Adede lives with her tribe, making sure she has enough food for herself and her children. Cooperating with the tribe is one of the greatest tools for her survival because everyone looks out for each other and protects one another from predators and rival tribes.

One day, she is given some food by a friend. Let's say it was mixed nuts and seeds, like some kind of ancient muesli. Delicious. Later that day, she's out picking berries and trips on a tree root and falls, hurting her leg; luckily, nothing is broken and she survives. What she'll remember from that day isn't the kind gesture and the tasty muesli, but the fall, simply because that event could have led, eventually, to her death. She has to remember to be more careful on that route to ensure it doesn't happen again. She might even tell the story around the fire to the rest of the tribe as a warning. The muesli, meanwhile, will never get a mention.

Okay, but why is this? Since negative experiences, such as getting injured, were potentially life-threatening, our brains developed to store and recall them in order to keep us alive. We have a built-in alarm system to aid this process: the amygdala, an almond-shaped region in each side of the brain that uses many of its neurons to quickly commit negative experiences to memory. Positive experiences are not stored in the same way as they are not essential to our survival. So our negativity bias is not our fault—our brains have developed this way in order to keep us alive.

This is not so helpful to us now, however. Most of us do not face the same threats as Adede did thousands of years ago: we are unlikely to die from the effects of a minor injury, for example. Dr. Hanson explains how in the modern world this negativity bias can give us "a growing sensitivity to stress, upset, and other negative experiences; a tendency toward pessimism, regret, and resentment; and long shadows cast by old pain."

Yet Dr. Hanson claims that there is a way to override this ancient reflex. He believes that we can train our brains so that instead of expecting the worst and despairing, we come to expect the best and become more hopeful.

try this:
BRAIN TRAINING

The next time something good happens, allow yourself to enjoy the positive feelings that occur and try to stay with them for a few moments—taking in the experience and the detail of what you can see, smell, taste, and hear. By focusing on these warm, joyful, fulfilling emotions and sensations, the situation is more likely to stay with us by transferring to our long-term memory.

We can also do this by remembering a recent time when something went right. By staying with that memory, lingering there for a while, and enjoying it, this too will then transfer to a long-term memory.

If you're like me and enjoy a hands-on creative type of exercise, you might like to create a scrap board, collage or photo album of images—maybe even a special album on your phone—that reminds you of times when you have experienced happiness or hope. Use the pictures to trigger a joyful recent memory, then stay with it so that it transfers to your long-term recall. These positive memories can make us feel more hopeful about the potential for joyful experiences in the future, especially if we usually tend toward a more negative outlook.

Reminding ourselves of enjoyable times past can help, no doubt, but this might only be part of the solution, especially if we feel like we're trapped in the Snow Queen's castle, unable to see any joy or an end to our pain. I know people living with debilitating depression and I have suffered from anxiety myself. Like so many of us, I have felt paralyzed by fear, unable to see a way out of my money worries, with threats of homelessness and mounting debts piling up. Some days it was easy to feel defeated before I'd even woken up properly or that I'd been plunged into a "pit of despair"—an awful and lonely place to be. I am all too aware of how sometimes the simplest action, such as taking a shower or stepping out of the house, can be an act of tremendous courage, which might leave us feeling as though there isn't much space for brain training or active hope. And we're by no means alone in this.

According to the 2014 NHS Adult Psychiatric Morbidity Survey, around one in six adults (17 percent) surveyed in England met the criteria for a common mental disorder (CMD) such as anxiety or depression. In the U.S., according to the National Alliance on Mental Illness, one in twenty-five U.S. adults experience serious mental illness each year, with suicide being the second leading cause of death among people aged ten to thirty-four. According to those statistics, there's a high probability that each one of us knows someone who struggles with their mental health or that we're struggling with our own.

To find out more, I spoke with two NHS psychiatric nurses, Natalie and Ian, who have chalked up over forty years of experience between them. I wanted to hear how professionals with hands-on experience and expertise find hope for themselves and their patients.

Natalie—who also happens to be my sister—told me that the big change in the last few years has been an increase in people needing or wanting referrals, "especially in men, with many more having suicidal thoughts." This chimes with the 2012 survey by the Office for National Statistics (UK), which shows the highest suicide rate to be among men aged forty-five to forty-nine, while in the U.S. 75 percent of people who die by suicide are male.

Remarking on the statistics, mental health charity MIND said,

"It appears that how people cope with mental health problems is getting worse as the number of people who self-harm or have suicidal thoughts is increasing." Whether that's because more of us are ready to be open about our experiences or because there are simply more of us having these issues—or both—is open to debate. Natalie believes that the stresses of modern life are a contributing factor, particularly social media, which has become a place "where we are encouraged to fear and hate each other... None of that is helpful or conducive to positive mental health. If you are already anxious, depressed, or vulnerable and you are exposed to negative messages, to terrifying stories, to impossible standards—bombarded by images and messages of what you should look like and how your life should be—these things will only make you feel much worse." This, combined with the fact that many people have also been affected by other factors such as austerity, economic downturn, concerns about the environmental crisis, job losses, and the many other worries brought on by the 2020 global pandemic, inevitably means that people feel as though "their safety nets have been removed," as Natalie put it.

When we're feeling this way, one of the most difficult things can be knowing where or how to ask for help, which means that often people don't realize that their friend or family member is suffering under a burden. This is partly down to the particularly stubborn stigma around mental health, meaning that people are afraid to open up, not knowing that other people feel this way too. Thankfully, this has started to change.

On November 20, 2018, Prince William took part in a discussion at the This Can Happen conference, which promotes mental health support in the workplace. He spoke candidly about his own mental health struggles and how "very sad and very down" he became when working as an air ambulance pilot and was faced with a traumatic incident involving children. He said that being able to talk with his crew helped him to come to terms with "the enormous sadness of what I witnessed." When we see a prince—or a professional athlete, musician, or actor—discussing their challenges and admitting that they've felt sad or anxious and in need of support, it helps us to see that we don't have to pretend to be okay when we are very much *not* okay.

try this:
YOUR SUPPORT NETWORK

Creating and maintaining a support network for yourself is vital to maintaining positive mental health so you don't have to face enormous challenges alone. Even if you're not in crisis right now, take the opportunity to prepare so you'll be able to easily get the help you might need should you find yourself having a difficult time in the future.

Write a list of people in your support network. Take time to consider who is best for different scenarios (this may be more than one person, of course). For example: someone to cheer you up or to have fun with; someone who is great at listening and will just let you talk; someone who can help you to make decisions or solve problems in practical ways; someone who can look after you when you can't look after yourself. You may want to list people for other categories that apply to your life and problems you've encountered in the past (someone who you can stay with, who can offer financial support, who can give technical advice, etc.). Make sure you have up-to-date contact information for all these people so you can get in touch easily.

It may be that writing this list makes you realize you don't have all the people you need, but this is okay too.

When new people appear in your life, it will help you recognize that they are exactly what you were looking for—and that you can be a support for them too. Building a support network takes time.

Finally, when you are in a crisis, make sure you do reach out to the relevant people on your list. If you feel scared or nervous at the prospect of asking for help, it's worth remembering this: every single person in the world will need help at some point in their lives, and people who care about you would much rather you asked for their help than suffer alone.

Being able to discuss things openly is such an important part of regaining hope. Despite her criticisms of social media, Natalie does feel that posts by well-known figures speaking about their mental health struggles have helped encourage "the floodgates to open" in a positive way—with more people seeking the help they need. She told me:

> *Hope comes when someone is allowed to express their fears and will not be ridiculed for doing so. As soon as they voice their fears, there is hope, because that means that they are reaching out. By doing so, they are saying "I feel like this, can you help me feel better?" And then we will try to find a way. Hope lies in the connections between people.*

Ian agreed, adding:

> *Sometimes it's as simple as being able to talk about tomorrow. If you can do that, I see that as a marker of hope, because talking about it means that for that person there will be a tomorrow. We have to help people find hope in the short, medium, and long term.*

try this:
TAKING OUR TIME

If you have a friend who seems down, look for a space and opportunity for you to chat with them and listen. Don't worry about getting it "wrong," and don't feel as though you have to "fix" them or offer unsolicited solutions to their problems. Instead, just listen, without interruption, to what they have to say. You can ask them what they need or if there is anything you can do if this feels right. Make sure they know that you care and that you're there for them. Having someone by our side can in itself help us feel less lonely and more hopeful. If your friend needs professional help, they might also welcome your support in taking that next step.

Finding your way out of a serious mental health issue is never going to be easy. Nevertheless, Natalie believes that there are some really key things that we can all do as individuals to help ourselves and each other feel more hopeful on our darkest days. Once again, kindness is central:

Some people have bought into the narrative that they are rubbish. But it's not true: we are all good enough. We have to learn to be compassionate toward ourselves and each other... Sometimes it is enough to remember that if you're alive, you are winning. Just keep breathing.

try this:
BE KIND TO YOUR SELF

Check in with yourself several times every day, as you might with a good friend, and ask yourself how you're feeling. You only need a moment, but if there are feelings of sadness or anxiety bubbling under, you can take steps to help yourself feel better before those feelings get worse.

Refer back to your Wellness Toolbox in chapter one. Ask yourself if you're making time for those vital things that make you happy and keep you well. Take a moment to remind yourself of some of the exercises we've explored so far: Are there a couple that you've found especially helpful? If so, bring those back into your everyday.

By "checking in" with kindness, I find that I notice when I need a break before I get really exhausted and risk despair taking hold. I'm able to take a short walk in the park at lunchtime and to take a few deep breaths while focusing on nothing else but this. This simple daily practice has really helped me keep well and maintain hope.

Talking with Natalie and Ian about their jobs was immensely humbling. Natalie admits that she suffers terribly when she sadly loses patients from suicide, as does occasionally happen.

We have helped thousands of people to see hope and another day, and yet we tend to remember only the ones who didn't make it. We must all remember the others, the ones who did make it. Our jobs are ultimately about life.

Although Natalie often sees people on "their worst days," she also sees them at their best, rediscovering hope out of despair. And this not only applies to patients but to her NHS colleagues too, who "see awful things and experience grief and sadness, and yet still the next day they get up, no matter what, determined to help the next person who needs them."

try this:
SOMETHING TO LOOK FORWARD TO

If you've had an especially difficult day (or a series of them), give yourself one thing to look forward to tomorrow, and think about this before you go to sleep. It needn't be much: a cup of hot chocolate, a chance to catch up with a friend, a long bath, rewatching one of your favorite movies. Sometimes having even just a small treat planned can gently deliver us through difficult days and give us hope: "Tomorrow will be better as I have this to look forward to."

It is essential for us to acknowledge that we all need to talk about mental health more. There have definitely been steps in the right direction, but we collectively need to be as open as we can about our suffering, to show people that they don't have to go through it alone, to help them and ourselves find hope for tomorrow. When times are tough, money is short, and troubles are plentiful, it can feel as though hope has also been lost, but there is *always* something we can hold on to. And focusing on this something shows us that there is light in the dark. Each day brings new gifts, and knowing this to be true gives us hope that the future—tomorrow, next week, next year, and beyond—will bring the same.

CHAPTER FOUR
finding the light

STAYING HOPEFUL THROUGH DEATH AND GRIEF

....

"THAT IT WILL NEVER COME AGAIN
IS WHAT MAKES LIFE SO SWEET."

—EMILY DICKINSON

THERE'S AN OLD FABLE ABOUT a man who is chased by a ferocious beast into a well. At its bottom is a dragon. The man clings on to a branch in the wall of the well, which is being slowly gnawed away by two mice, one black and one white. The man reaches out and tastes two drops of honey he spots on the other side of the well. He keeps clinging on to the branch, as the beast prowls, and the dragon roars, and the mice gnaw away at the branch.

The Russian novelist Leo Tolstoy retells this folk story in his autobiographical book "My Confession." In his version, the protagonist is not able to enjoy the honey because of the inevitability of death. Tolstoy then explores this dilemma: How can we enjoy our lives when death—the dragon with an open mouth below us—is a certainty? In one of the responses Tolstoy describes, he presents the importance of living the good life with the time we have, while being fully aware that life is ephemeral.

Understanding and finding meaning in death is a journey driven by an existential crisis familiar to many of us. We may question the point of doing anything if we're all going to die in the end, or feel that our efforts are worthless because they'll disappear along with our minds. Or, as my friend Lucy Nicholls joked, "What's the point if all my life amounts to is how many episodes of *The Real Housewives of Orange County* I have watched?"

Our response to death varies for many reasons, including our belief systems, cultural backgrounds, and personal philosophies. In multi-faith, multicultural nations such as the United Kingdom and the United States, many different traditions around death are practiced. If your faith means that you believe in an afterlife in paradise, your hope may lie in a "better place" for you and your loved ones after death, and that might help you accept the inevitable end of your time on earth.

However, in the British Social Attitudes survey carried out in 2018, 52 percent of people declared themselves as having no religion, while in the U.S., according to the Religious Landscape Study, 22.8 percent of people say the same. If you don't have the consolation of faith and don't or can't believe in the possibility of arriving in heaven with your consciousness fully intact, perhaps your hope lies in science. The first law of thermodynamics says that energy can neither be created nor destroyed, only transferred or changed from one form to another. So the energy in our bodies is released when we decompose, becoming energy for the earth to use in the form of nutrients for the soil. And new life springs forth.

Over 4.5 million years ago, in previous generations of stars, all the carbon, nitrogen, and oxygen atoms in our bodies were created—we are literally made of stars. Roughly five billion years from now, earth will likely have vaporized when our dying sun expands into a red giant and engulfs our planet. Then all matter will "return to sender," with all our stardust returning to the universe. In his 1980 television series *Cosmos*, the astrologist Carl Sagan famously said: "Some part of our being knows this is where we came from. We long to return. And we can, because the cosmos is also within us. We're made of star stuff. We are a way for the cosmos to know itself."

Poets, songwriters, dreamers, and scientists all loved this notion. It was, and is, incredibly hopeful; it connects us to the entire universe, infinite and mysterious.

Although I don't relish the idea of being dead, I find comfort in the idea that my physical body can be put to good use, can help grow something or feed something, and eventually become part of the cosmic recycling scheme. It gives me hope that, in a very real, tangible way, I will continue.

Of course, not everyone will be comforted by this notion. You might consider it all very well for your body to break down, but what about "you"? What about your mind, your thoughts, all the things you've learned, considered, or imagined? And even if your beliefs *do* include the notion of an afterlife, this doesn't necessarily mean being free from the pain and hopelessness that the certainty of death, and possible suffering, can sometimes bring.

Fear of death is common—and natural. Nevertheless, I'd like us to consider some of the ways in which we might stay hopeful in the face of it. And to begin by specifically considering hope as related to our fears and anxieties around our own deaths.

When we think about the fact of our mortality and the unbearable truth of our finite nature, it can be overwhelming. However, as our life expectancies have improved, alongside the treatment of disease and mortality rates in childbirth and infancy, death has generally become less "present" for many of us. Today we're much less likely to witness a person dying than we were in times past. Yet I wonder if this has also made it more frightening to confront and accept the reality.

During the coronavirus pandemic, suddenly it seemed as though we were being confronted by death at every turn—for the first time for many of us. Those with long-term health conditions (including asthmatic me) or those deemed part of the "at risk" group were acutely reminded of our fragility. As my neighbor said, "Every moment the news is telling me I am going to die." As the death count rose, claiming people of all ages, including many who were previously perfectly healthy, we became increasingly aware of our own mortality. The pandemic revealed how little we talk about death and how ill prepared we are to face it. For many of us, death and dying are unmentionable subjects, or at least deeply uncomfortable ones, but being open to beginning these conversations can be a first step toward living with the knowledge of our own mortality. We can do this and still hold on to the hope that we can enjoy our lives right now, and the certainty of death needn't take that away from us.

try this:
TIME AND SPACE TO THINK

Check in with yourself for a moment before we continue. Ask yourself how you feel about death. You don't need to do anything else just yet but give yourself some time and space to pay attention to the thoughts and emotions that arise and to how they make you feel. Be kind and gentle with yourself. If this exercise brings up any fear or anxiety, remind yourself that right now, you are alive and you are safe. If you feel able to read on, I really hope that this chapter will help you. Take it slow.

In 2017, I began working on a theater show about the fear of death, aptly titled *The Death Show*, with artists Antonia Beck and Lucy Nicholls. Antonia and Lucy first met at a work function, and then, over a cup of tea, a cranberry muffin, and a bit of small talk, happened to discover they were both terrified of death. (This phobia has a name: "thanatophobia," after the Greek god Thanatos, related to both Nyz, his mother and the goddess of night, and to Hypnos, his brother and the god of sleep.) Right there and then they decided to make a show that would examine why we "struggle to accept our own mortality."

They set about doing some practical and comprehensive research around the subject, partaking in a celebrant training course, spending time at a funeral director's, and speaking with patients living with terminal illnesses at a hospice. They prepared a dead body and witnessed the unconcealed process of cremation. They were moved by the tenderness of the funeral home staff, who wanted to make sure that every single person received proper care and dignity and that their grieving families were well looked after. They investigated exactly what occurs to our physical bodies at the moment of death—and then afterward—and considered what happens to our consciousness or what many people call our souls.

By becoming more familiar with all these stages and processes, they hoped to confront and assuage their fear of death; they wanted to figure out why they were so afraid, and what they could do about it, before sharing that knowledge with others.

Lucy and Antonia told me:

We've come to realize that a big part of living a full and hopeful life is acknowledging death. Talking about it and taking action, so that

we feel more informed about what our end-of-life choices might be.
After all, if we know that we're all going to die, then let's talk about it.

They said that being able to speak about death with our own friends and families means a better chance of us having a "good death," which has helped them to become more comfortable with the whole notion. Being as prepared as possible can enable us to have the experience we wish for at the end of our lives: to be with the people we want around us, to have the objects and music we love with us, to be in the most ideal of circumstances. These discussions can also help our funerals be a little easier for our loved ones—both practically and emotionally. By starting this conversation, you will hopefully encourage others to talk about their preferences too.

I asked Nikki, a palliative care nurse with decades of experience in end-of-life care, for her thoughts on this. Nikki told me that the most important thing to remember is that everyone is different. What each person needs and wants is as individual as they are, and some people are ready and willing to talk and plan for death and dying while others are less so, and that people's opinions on the subject can change. She said death plans were like birth plans: "You may plan for a home birth in a pool, and when the times comes you get a caesarean in a hospital, because that was what was needed." Nikki also spoke with me about how, even at the end, we can find hope:

On a bad day, when the patient feels that everything is awful, I just ask, "What could I do right now to make this moment a little bit better? Could I get you a drink or hold your hand?" Hope doesn't have to be about the long-term future or about planning a massive funeral. It could just be a spark of hope for the moment that you are in, with something as simple as a visit from a family member.

I found this so encouraging and it seems like something any of us can do for each other, to simply ask, "What can I do to make it better right now?" Hopefully we can be brave enough, when the time comes, to let people know how they could help us to have the best moment possible, in the time and the circumstances available.

try this:
THE BIG CONVERSATION

You might now feel able to start a conversation with your loved ones about what you hope for in relation to your own death—and to ask them what they might hope for in their own.

Go extremely gently: most people find it difficult to begin talking about this stuff, so you might find some resistance. If they're not ready, don't push. Instead, let them know that you're available whenever they want to talk.

If they are open to the conversation, chat about what

kind of funeral you might like and ask them about their thoughts too. It's also important to talk about how you'd like to die—in what kind of setting, your wishes about different medical interventions and end-of-life care—as well as what you'd like to happen to the things you'll leave behind and to your body. It's sure to feel a little uncomfortable, and you may stumble over your words or thoughts, but you'll find your way through—I promise. It can also be a really special opportunity to share how much you care for one another and what you'd like to do together in the rest of your lives.

Eventually, Antonia and Lucy's theater show came to be about a life well lived, rather than a show about death. While their research didn't assuage their fears completely, it helped them to realize the importance of getting on with having the best life you can and enjoying it as much as humanly possible, especially the small and simple pleasures. For Lucy and Antonia, that included things like chocolate trifles, looking at pictures of baby gibbons, swimming in the sea, and a nice glass of wine.

Writer and bon vivant Charles Bukowski said, "We are here to laugh at the odds and live our lives so well that death will tremble to take us." Maybe this is where our hope can also lie: in living our lives so incredibly well that fear of our own death begins to loosen its grip a little. So that when the Grim Reaper approaches—and is good enough to give us a bit of notice—we can feel contented that we've done what we wanted with our allotted time. In Terry Pratchett's excellent literary multiverse, Death is a scythe-carrying skeleton gentleman in a hooded cape who speaks IN CAPITAL LETTERS and is quietly regretful about his inevitability. Imagine for a moment that we could see him traipsing around after us all the time. Might this visual reminder make us live our lives differently?

We all know deep down that none of us will be on our death-beds regretting that we didn't buy more shoes or do more admin. Yet, as my friend Ibrahim said when considering this thought, "If I literally lived every day like it was my last, I would be in a police cell for causing a public disturbance for anarchic break dancing in Lewisham High Street." (No judgment here; to each their own). I don't want anyone to get arrested, of course, but I do invite you to consider what you actively hope to do with your one wonderful life.

try this:
BEFORE I DIE

This exercise is inspired by the global art project of the same name. The artist Candy Chang creates contempo-rary memento mori (the term for an artistic or symbolic reminder of death's inevitability) in the form of walls in community or public spaces, where people are invited to chalk up their responses to the sentence "Before I die, I want to..."

Write down a list of what you want to do before you die. Add to it whenever you think of something new. We don't know when our day will come, so get cracking with your list right now and make plans to put it into action. Keep your list with you and try to do one of the smaller, more manageable things on your list every day.

If there are no small, manageable things on your list, create some! The small things are very important in living a fulfilling life day-to-day, not just during the major events we plan for. Maybe you want to dance in your kitchen, go for a walk on the beach, or bake a ridiculously rich cake. It's about making sure that in each day we make some space for joy. Hope lies in the joy we squeeze out of life before death comes.

Our fear of death can come in other forms, of course. For some people it's not what happens to their body or "themselves" that worries them: it's the fear of being forgotten. It's a notion that has obsessed many folk throughout history, determined to leave behind a legacy that will help their memory live on.

Interviewers often ask famous people, "How would you like to be remembered?" The answer is usually something like "as someone who always made people laugh." The thing is, while a famous person might expect to leave behind a bit of a longer trail, the lives of most of us will fade from view pretty quickly.

Still, I believe that each of us does continue to live on, in a way, even if no one knows exactly who we were. None of us remembers our Stone Age ancestors, but they exist in our DNA and through our progress, our inventions, our beliefs. No one knows the name of the Mesopotamian potter who invented the wheel 5,500 years ago, but we still cherish it and acknowledge it as a key advance. We live on through our actions, through what we did in the world, and the influence this continues to have on others beyond even our families. If we can try to accept ourselves as one small but vital part of an ecosystem of thought and life, then being remembered in a literal way might not matter so much after all.

And, of course, we will be remembered, for a while at least. Those who loved us, or were connected to us, will tell our stories and keep their memories of our time together. Once the last person who remembers us or notes our achievements is gone, we—as individuals at least—are gone also. If we have children, however, we live on by way of our DNA, maybe even past the point at which we're remembered as individuals, if our descendants continue to have children of their own. Who knows where your passion for music first began? Or from whom you inherited your calming presence or creative flair? A distinctive nose or a specific family phrase could easily go back multiple generations.

try this:
FORGET-ME-NOT

Think about how you would hope to be remembered and get creative with it. You could make a film on your phone, write some letters or poems, even a biography you could add to over the coming years. You could make a memory book with favorite recipes, jokes, or songs—whatever's important to you and gives the best sense of who you are.

Also, consider this. We often focus on the strongest impression a person gave while living: Grandad was funny, Nana was a great poet, Mrs. Hibdidge was a brilliant storyteller, Uncle David threw amazing parties, Malcolm never had a bad word to say about anyone. If you'd hope to be described as "funny" or "kind" or "generous" after your death, then act on that hope. Be funny, be kind, be generous today.

I was surprised to discover while working on *The Death Show* that I'm not scared of death at all, even though I'm scared of other things that are comparatively harmless, such as life-size puppets and the skin on custard. This intrigued me, but I realized that I'm not afraid of death in the same way that I am not afraid of flying. Other people worry about the plane crashing, but I know there is nothing I can do to stop that happening, apart from not getting on board in the first place. Yet while I'm not scared of death itself or about how long I'm remembered for, it's much harder for me to muster hope in the face of illness, suffering, pain, and grief, those things that so often accompany death.

Most people want to die in their sleep. No one wants a protracted and painful illness, but sadly, too many people will have this experience. Facing death when it comes to us in this way is very different from knowing that death is coming for us *eventually*. But just because our time has arrived, it doesn't mean that we have to give up hope completely. We can find a way to greet death that does justice to the way we have lived our lives.

The social artist R. M. Sanchez-Camus describes death as the "last taboo"—something that he realized during his time working in hospices creating beautiful artwork with the dying. When he mentioned where he worked and with whom, he noticed how some people recoiled. But he also learned that "nobody wants to live as much as the dying," recognizing the huge benefits of being creative at this point in our lives. Making something beautiful, having purpose, and being included is missing for many people in their final weeks, but it can be a way of being hopeful right until the very end. The artworks Sanchez-Camus cocreates with the dying are beautiful, defiant expressions of lives lived well.

Perhaps another way to hold hope, even when we know death

to be edging closer, is to find a purpose, a way to give meaning to our last days by accomplishing one final thing.

Ian Toothill was introduced to me by a mutual friend. He'd been diagnosed with bowel cancer in 2015 and, against all odds, had beaten it. A very short while after we first met, it came back, and Ian was told that he only had a few months to live. Unsurprisingly, he was devastated by the news. I couldn't imagine how you would even begin to process the grief and anger of cancer returning just when you thought you were over it.

Next thing I heard, Ian was planning on climbing Mount Everest, to try to become the first person with cancer to reach the summit and raise a lot of money for Macmillan Cancer Support. Like many others, I helped as much and as often as I could. Pledges came flooding in. I spoke to Ian just before he left. He'd faced a lot of hurdles before he'd even begun: organizing insurance; assembling an experienced team who would have the courage to climb with a terminally ill man, as no one climbs Everest alone; speaking with health professionals to give himself the best chance of making it.

Ian told me the preparation and the fundraising had pulled him through his darkest days: "It gave me a purpose, and that always helps, just having something to focus on, that keeps you going, so I didn't have to think about being ill all the time."

Then he was off. I had daily updates on Ian's progress. I heard how the storms got so bad that some team members retired and that Ian's tent got destroyed, but he persevered. On June 5, 2017, he reached the summit, planting a Sheffield United football team flag in the snow, despite being a lifelong fan of their rivals, Sheffield Wednesday, because a friend had promised to donate £1,000 if he did so.

At Ian's funeral, many people talked about how much he had inspired them and had given them hope that it was possible to achieve anything if you persevered. On the anniversary of his climb, a group of his friends scattered his ashes on Ben Nevis in Scotland.

I am so glad I knew Ian, even for a short while. I still think about him and his Everest climb whenever I feel a bit defeated. I remember what he said about the power of finding a purpose. As he told me himself, his strength was bolstered by the encouragement he received from friends and supporters, and because he had a single, definite, and tangible aim. Ian had no hope of getting better, but he did have hope that he'd make it to the summit.

Of course, not all of us could climb Everest with the knowledge that our time left is limited. But we could all find comfort in a purpose, which might be as simple as making a list of all the old friends you'd like to speak with and then reconnecting with them, one by one, writing a series of letters to each of your loved ones, recording the story of your life in words or pictures, or it could be painting a beautiful picture, creating an intricate mosaic, making a playlist for people to remember you by, recording a series of stories for your grandchildren, or planting bulbs in a garden which might live on after you've gone. To find an achievable project could be a valuable act of self-care at this time, no matter how big or small, and can give you something to focus on and take joy in.

My friend Chahine died of a particularly aggressive type of lung cancer last year. He had an amazing life full of adventures and friends, travels, and creativity. He was a polymath but best known for being a theater lighting designer. Every time we worked on a show together, he would say to me, "Make sure you find your light," as I was highly skilled at standing where I couldn't be seen, which is a fairly big error when you're in a performance that people are paying to see.

His illness was painful and protracted: the cancer left and then came back "with friends," as he said. He got thinner and became pale, had a baffling number of tablets to take, as well as countless appointments and challenging treatments. But Chahine decided he was still going to enjoy himself, even once he was moved into a hospice, where he told me stories of his room full of friends and bottles of Prosecco, raucous laughter, storytelling, reminiscences, and love. Chahine invited everyone he loved to spend time with into his room at the hospice, although he wasn't afraid to say when he wanted to be left alone. His funeral was a firework display on a barge, where we could all hear his recorded voice booming out through the PA system, prompting my friend to remark affectionately: "Trust Chahine, what a bastard. Not one of us will have a funeral to match that." Poets and long-lost relatives read out words and memories dedicated to him. Chahine set a standard for us all, of how to live and how to die.

His friends set a very high standard on how to put on a funeral too. All of it—his life, his death, even his funeral—were underpinned by hopefulness.

We can all achieve this too, I believe, by asking for what we want for those final days, allowing ourselves to be surrounded as much as possible by the people and things that bring us happiness.

The way Ian and Chahine approached the end fills me with hope that it's possible not to give in to despair. But for many of us, facing our own end isn't nearly as awful as facing the loss of a loved one in the knowledge that their time with us is limited. It's incredibly hard to witness and to care for someone who might be suffering. The physical symptoms and emotional toll can weigh heavily on your spirits; finding and holding on to hope through these days can be especially painful or even feel impossible.

If you are looking after someone who is ill, sometimes the best you can do is keep them company. And if the pain, the worry, and the treatments are exhausting and frightening and relentless, the act of caring and loving is sometimes the best we can do. Yet, if there is the briefest moment of respite from discomfort, a moment of peace and quiet, there is often the possibility here for more: for fun, laughter, conversation, entertainment.

My friend Damon looked after his husband, Angel, when there was no longer any chance of him recovering from cancer, and I spoke to him about whether hope can be found when someone is dying. He said that even when all hope was gone, "beauty was always there, in actions and in nature, and was the only thing that gave me solace. Beauty always intrudes when there is no hope."

I thought this was an incredible thing to say.

I kept company with my friend Anna when she was dying, and we spent some time looking out of her hospital window at the birds on the telephone wires. It was a nice distraction: she didn't want to talk about being ill and I had no idea what to say about it either, but we enjoyed watching the birds, trying to remember which was which, looking out for shapes in the clouds, taking in the way the light moved across the buildings. It was a moment of peace, when we both were able to take pleasure in what surrounded us at a really dark time. To accept that death is coming to someone you love, and soon—and how you even begin to process that, to bear it—is so, so hard. There is comfort to be had in the fact that life goes on and that they are still with us even after they die—in our memories, in what they taught us, in what we learned from them, the things they loved and shared with us and showed us how to appreciate. And there is comfort too in the love we still feel for them—which is, of course, also the source of our grief.

Grieving takes time. And it takes a different amount of time for everyone; it can't be rushed. Over the centuries, different cultures have given a variety of allotted times for grieving, as if grief can be measured equally for all of us, allowing us one portion each over a certain amount of time. I can see how this may be useful for some people, and how it would have been devised with compassion (so we don't get lost in grief) and for practical reasons (we have to get the harvest in, for example). However, today we live in different times and circumstances, in which the older rules may not be so helpful or useful. So maybe we have to create a new set of ideas for how we might deal with grief today. Of course, everyone experiences grief differently: advice from terminal illness charity Marie Curie on how to be a good friend to someone who is grieving includes: letting them know you're thinking about them, however you can; when you talk to them, bear in mind that you don't know how they're feeling, so take your lead from them, as they may or may not want to talk; and if you knew the person they're grieving for, saying something kind about them can be very comforting too.

David Harradine and Sam Butler are co-artistic directors of the arts company Fevered Sleep. When David's sister died completely unexpectedly in a car crash, he saw his parents having "the most horrible time because none of their friends or relatives knew how to deal with their grief." Someone his mum had known her whole life "ran away from her in the supermarket rather than saying that impossible thing: 'I am sorry your daughter's dead.'" David found his friends were incredibly supportive at first but that "people stopped talking to me about it way before I'd even gotten over the initial shock." He told Sam how angry this made him and that he wished he could wear a T-shirt saying: "I am still grieving. Why have you stopped talking to me about it?" Sam's response was that's a great idea.

Together Sam and David created This Grief Thing, using empty shops as a venue in which people could come together to discuss grief and loss. These pop-up shops sold T-shirts, sweatshirts, and other items bearing expressions collected from the 150 or so people with whom they had spoken, such as "Grief = Love" and "Don't Panic If I Cry." These clothes are our twenty-first-century equivalent of a black armband: expressions of loss worn on our bodies so that people can know our circumstances, and which also serve as conversation-starters when someone asks, "Why does your T-shirt say 'Let Me Be Sad'?" David and Sam's aim is to help us all get better at thinking about, talking about, and understanding grief.

I asked David if he thought there could be any hope in the midst of grief, and this was his response:

> *What I have come to learn is that grief never goes away. I don't want it to because my grief is what my love for my sister turned into. I will always love her, so I don't want to stop grieving, but I have come to realize that my grief easily coexists with extreme joy and wild hope.*

Allowing yourself to experience "wild hope" like that which David found is, I believe, to accept and recognize that joy, grief, and sadness can and do coexist. It is about acknowledging the complexity of our emotions around loss, of not fearing the darkness of anger and pain and suffering while seeking the light of future happiness and enjoyable remembrance. Wild hope is about allowing ourselves to have faith in the fact that even in the midst of the suffering that comes with grief, there is a day coming when it won't hurt so deeply and that there will even be days when the pain is replaced by fond remembering that does not diminish our love for the ones we have lost. Wild hope is about living our lives well as the best way of honoring those who can no longer do so.

Our response to death is part of what makes us human, and our grieving process is as individual as we are. Yet there are many similarities too. In 2005, David Kessler and Elisabeth Kubler outlined the five stages of grief they had identified in their book *On Grief and Grieving*, written to help readers learn to live with loss and to understand and identify what we may be feeling. These stages are: denial (which helps us to survive the initial shock); anger (which we must allow ourselves to feel so that it can dissipate); bargaining (which could be a type of "magical thinking" when we try to wish the person back to life or wellness); depression (an appropriate response to a great loss and an important part of the healing process); and acceptance (not the same as being "okay," but allowing ourselves to live a full life again once we have given grief its time).

Kessler and Kubler were clear that we don't all go through these stages in the same order, nor in a linear way. Nevertheless, many people have found great comfort in their work. The most useful thing I have learned from them is the importance of self-compassion in grief—and to recognize that the journey is individual. We must be gentle with ourselves and grant the stages of grief—whatever they are for us—enough time for us to heal. There is also help out there:

organizations such as Mental Health America offer bereavement support and advice. Death Cafés offer informal spaces for people to gather and discuss their experiences in a safe space. We don't have to be alone in our grief if we don't wish to be.

I think back now to Chahine telling me to "find the light." I like to think he was really talking about finding the light—the hope—in life; in death; in the world around us and everything in it, including our losses and pain and sadness, because of the immense connected beauty of the whole universe and everything in it. Or he might have just been telling me to stop wriggling around and to stay on my mark onstage.

Ultimately, we can try to stay healthy but we can still get sick; we can cross the road with caution but a car might still swerve around the corner at high speed. Whatever we think happens next, we also have to work on our acceptance of death, which comes, I think, by talking about it openly and preparing for it as best we can, hand-in-hand with those we love. Death is humbling, and all we can hope for—and act upon—is to live as well and as brightly as possible, so that we're able to die in the knowledge that we did our very best, and that is a beautiful and honorable intention. It is all we should expect of ourselves and each other, and it is plenty.

CHAPTER FIVE

murmurations

REAPING THE BENEFITS
OF COMMUNITY CONNECTIONS

....

"YE CANNOT LIVE FOR YOURSELVES;
A THOUSAND FIBERS CONNECT YOU
WITH YOUR FELLOW-MEN."

—HENRY MELVILL

HE ANCIENT GREEK PHILOSOPHER ARISTOTLE said we
humans are "by nature a social animal." Over two thousand
years later, neuroscientists are coming to the same conclusion: we
crave connection with each other, and our need to connect is as
fundamental as our need for food and water.

Matthew D. Lieberman is a professor of social cognitive neuroscience at UCLA. His studies and experiments concerning the inter-
face between brain science and human behavior have led him to
conclude that the "social pain" we may experience when our connections are threatened or severed (such as when we are snubbed at
a party, ignored by a colleague, or excluded from an activity) is "a

sign that evolution has treated social connection as a necessity, not a luxury." In other words, we are hardwired to seek out connection with others in order to survive.

Because of the ways in which we live and work today, we are in danger of losing some of the traditional connections that help us, both practically and emotionally. When working long hours or desperately trying to fit in the many tasks of the day, we are all vulnerable to feeling isolated and lonely, with less time to meet and interact with others. As a species, we need this vital social contact—a fact that was immediately apparent during the pandemic lockdown. Suddenly the need to self-isolate severed many of our normal ways of connecting. It came as a shock to many who struggled to adapt. What was heartening, however, was the inventive ways that people found to reach out to one another, with ideas of how to do so being shared across the world: the kids using walkie-talkies to speak to their pals across the street, families employing technology to enjoy a virtual Sunday lunch, residents of apartment blocks singing as one, groups of people exercising together on their own doorsteps, and messages of encouragement chalked on pavements—these all helped hope to blossom as people overcame the limitations of social distancing.

Now more than ever, it is time to celebrate our interdependence rather than our individualism. There are so many ways to connect with the people around you and all of them are important. Not only do they allow us to survive, as Lieberman discovered, but they can help us to thrive. Put simply, connection and community can create and offer hope. You could start a new connection by simply speaking to a stranger on the subway or bus. The fact that this might feel like a radical suggestion is perhaps a sign of how out-of-practice some of us have become at reaching out. Nevertheless, you might be unsurprised to hear that I have a notable habit of starting conversations like this, which I discussed with siblings and campaigners George David Hodgson and Charlotte Hodgson on their mental health podcast *Talkin' About*.

Charlotte was surprised by my suggestion: "If you do speak to a stranger, they look at you like you're mad and they never talk back." But in my experience, they *do* talk back. Every time I speak to someone, they respond with very few exceptions (and usually these are because they think I'm trying to sell something). Since 2008, I have started conversations with strangers every time I travel in my city, as well as on trips around the country and beyond. I have concluded that people yearn to connect. I know I do.

When I boarded a bus recently, a boy, I reckon around thirteen years old, with a large cast on his right leg, wriggled out of my way so I could take the vacant seat next to him. I'd had a bad day up until that point—I hadn't gotten a job I'd applied for, I'd missed my dentist appointment, then I'd spilled boiling hot coffee on my trousers and broken a china teacup which belonged to my great aunt. Okay, not a tragic day, but a bit of a flattening one. But I smiled at the boy as I sat down. He smiled back.

Encouraged, I said, "Everyone in this bus will think I'm evil for making a poor boy with a broken leg get up just so I can sit down." He laughed and said, "Yes you are a bit evil," and then we both laughed together. I asked, "So, how did you break it?" and we chattered away from there. When we got onto the topic of drawing and painting, the elderly lady opposite us joined in as well. I got off at the next stop, and they were still chatting about art as the bus pulled away. That brief interaction really cheered me up. We three were complete strangers, different ages, with seemingly nothing in common except the bus journey and our city, but that didn't stop us from being kind to one another and connecting.

Of course, there will always be people who don't want to strike up a conversation for a myriad of reasons. I've done it thousands of times now, so I can usually tell who would welcome a chat or at least wouldn't mind one. But in general, I really believe that trying to connect is worth the risk of rejection, because the possible rewards of that encounter outweigh the possible downfalls (which do include, as Charlotte said, being "looked at as though you are mad"). These connections might transform a boring journey into an entertaining one. If you're having a tough day or are feeling isolated or lonely, these interactions can make things seem better, even if only briefly. They can remind you that you're not alone, that you can connect with others, that other people can be friendly, kind, amusing, interested, and interesting—and so can you.

try this:
HELLO STRANGER

Try to initiate one conversation in real life (not online) with a stranger in the next twenty-four hours. In recent times, as we donned masks and kept our distance to be safe during the pandemic, this was even more challenging than usual. Even so, we were still able to wave at each other, until such time when we are free to remove those masks and connect again, and try to chat.

Make sure when you do to be safe and sensible: don't approach someone down a dark Gotham City–esque alleyway filled with overspilling trash cans and wild-eyed stray cats; make sure you're in a public place in daylight, so you don't make people jump or get yourself in trouble.

A good way to open yourself up to new people and experiences is to choose someone who you might not normally talk with, even rejecting your initial choice.

In the first instance, just smile without expectation. If they don't smile back, then try not to take it personally; it could be for any number of reasons. Try someone else. If your smile is returned, try saying "Hello, how are you?" or ask if they've been waiting long or how old their kid is, did they see the game last night, or comment on how cold or sunny it is, how cute their dog is, or how nice their coat is. It's easy. I bet you'll be pleasantly surprised by how keen people are to chat.

I appreciate that this exercise is easier for some of us than others. As my friend John put it, "I'm a tall, funny-looking, gangly man. I can't go around smiling at strangers all day, they'd call the police." I'm aware it's a privilege of mine to be a fairly unthreatening person—small, middle-aged, white, and female—so this may not work for everyone. It almost goes without saying: please don't do it if it feels uncomfortable. Still, you might find that it's at least a good way of strengthening your connection with people in your neighborhood whom you already see regularly—neighbors, the postman, the person who serves you in the shop.

In these small moments, there is hope that we can all get along despite our superficial differences, that we don't have to be wary of everyone we meet. You don't even have to have a chat—a simple act of kindness such as returning a smile or giving someone your seat could brighten a person's day. With small, achievable actions, we can transform the world around us one bus journey at a time.

try this:
NOTICING KINDNESS

For the next twenty-four hours, when going about your daily life, focus on and take note of every time you witness an act of kindness or are its recipient. As we have explored previously, our "negativity bias" can influence what we recall, so focus on these moments in detail. Seeing for yourself that human beings are kind to one another, that strangers care about each other, that there is so much good happening in the world can all help a bud of hope to bloom.

You might choose to share these encounters with kindness on social media or tell your family and friends. I often share tales of real-life acts of kindness—either those that I've witnessed or tried myself—on social media. In my experience, people love hearing these stories. It's a small, powerful way of passing hope on.

Over the last few years, witnessing and completing daily acts of kindness has become one of my cornerstones of hope. I have come to realize that I can easily make a difference to someone and that a small act, such as helping carry heavy luggage, puts a smile on their face, gives me a buzz, and creates a momentary connection between us that is really enjoyable. If you have ever helped anyone out or supported them in times of trouble, then you too will know how good it feels. Neuroscience has shown that when we help others our brains release oxytocin, serotonin, and dopamine, often referred to as a "Helper's High." These hormones can make us feel happier and counter the effect of the stress hormone cortisol.

So take my seven-day kindness challenge and see how it feels! Keep a diary—not only of the acts themselves but of how you feel before, during, and after. This will help you to see if, and how, hope begins to flow.

try this:
SEVEN DAYS OF KINDNESS

Complete an act of kindness every day for one week. You will no doubt have your own amazing ideas, but here are seven suggestions to start you off.

Monday: Pay someone a compliment.

Tuesday: Write a thank-you letter to someone who has helped you in some way.

Wednesday: Tell somebody you love them and why (especially if you don't always get around to telling them often enough).

Thursday: Do a chore for someone so they don't have to—wash their car, take out the recycling, give them a break from childcare.

Friday: Contact someone you haven't spoken to for ages, who you know would be pleased to hear from you.

Saturday: Have a clear out and give away that dress or book or game that you know somebody else would really appreciate.

Sunday: Spend some quality time with a person you don't often get to see.

There's something really key about these small-scale encounters with kindness and what they can teach us about connection and hope. There are 7.5 billion of us alive right now (and counting)—and this can feel overwhelming when we want to make a difference in our globalized world. Nevertheless, if we can focus on the people around us right here and right now, connecting with the inhabitants of the particular piece we call home—both physically and online—this seems much more doable.

Making connections and forming relationships with our communities at a local level can be a hugely positive step. Most of us have friends and family, of course, but these days they are often scattered widely. Even if we're lucky to have them close by, the more connections we have, the better.

My own "little patch" is in Southeast London. I've lived here for twenty-odd years, and it has always been full of what my old history teacher Mr. Dennis would have called "colorful characters." It turns out some extraordinary people have lived and passed through here, and I find their stories full of hope: they were people just like you and me who became forces for good on their own doorsteps.

Octavia Hill (1838–1912) worked as a social reformer from the age of fourteen, despite having no formal education and growing up in poverty herself. She tried to create a public park on the site of diarist John Evelyn's manor house at Sayes Court, "to provide a place of beauty and fresh air for the people of Deptford in perpetuity." Although that endeavor was unsuccessful, she eventually went on to be one of the three founders of the National Trust. Another illustrious person with a connection to my area was Olaudah Equiano (c. 1745–1797), who was kidnapped as a child in Nigeria and sold to slave traders. He eventually bought his own freedom and became one of the leaders of the anti-slave-trade movement in the 1780s. My favorite, mainly because he was born in my street and because he has the most wonderful name ever, was Thankfull Sturdee (1852–1934). Despite his fairly humble background, he became the UK's first-ever press photographer, using his spare time to take portraits of ordinary local folk and their streets, documenting the dismal living conditions but also celebrating the brilliance and resilience of his community.

try this:
GO STORY HUNTING

What interests you about where you live? Start with a building, a street, or a name that really intrigues you. Follow that
lead and look into its history. Maybe you're wondering who
Tom Smith Close was named after. Or why that local park
was never built upon. Or what that old place on the corner
was originally conceived as. The way things look around us
now has so often been shaped by local people stepping in
and making things happen. It shows us that positive change
is possible and that history is full of stories of people acting
on their hopes and succeeding.

Some areas "give up" their stories more easily than others.
You could begin by visiting the archive of your local library,
museum, or history groups, but the best thing to do is to ask
your neighbors, particularly if they've been in the area for a
while. I've heard some great stories this way: street parties held
to celebrate the end of World War II; tug-of-war competitions
held as charity fundraisers by local firefighters; or empty buildings turned into artists' studios and galleries. Many of these tales
aren't recorded in history books. So get going, read, research,
and speak to people; it's a lovely way to connect with neighbors
and to discover some of your personal local heroes of hope.

Our local histories are fascinating, no doubt, but there are so many people standing up for the places they and their fellow residents call home today. In 2015, a consultation was announced to put in an AstroTurf pitch in Deptford Park, close to where I live. This would have replaced the existing football pitch, covered up the old athletic tracks, and reduced the natural green space, risking local wildlife.

A group of local people, who became known as DeptfordFolk, organized a meeting to discuss their opposition. Around fifty people showed up and, though they had no experience of how to go about it, managed to set up a park users' group and successfully persuade the council to reject the application. And they didn't stop there—they've started all sorts of initiatives, from installing benches to planting bulbs and trees and organizing an outdoor theater show. They recognized, in the words of their chair Trina Lynskey, that "parks are connected to the mental and physical health of residents, to wildlife, to pollution, to child poverty, to everything." And all of this sprang from a group of residents saying "no thanks" to an unwelcome change and hoping and acting for positive change instead.

try this:
PATCHWORK

Think about what you could do to improve your patch. What would make it a better place for you or your neighbors? Find out what's already going on, as sometimes the easiest, most efficient way to make a difference is simply to join in and support those who are already practicing active hope, perhaps volunteering at a food bank, helping to run an after-school sports club or visiting older people. Be realistic about what you can manage in terms of your time and other resources and also what you think you'd enjoy. Joining in with existing groups can make you feel more hopeful, reminding you that there are incredible people and projects already happening in your local area and succeeding in their aims.

If you've identified a goal but can't find an existing group for it, why not start one yourself? Begin small and check in with your local authority to find out if there are any funding opportunities or spaces that you could use for free.

Communities are stronger when working together, more able to protect and improve their environments, making them friendly, safe, and beautiful places to live. Groups of people can achieve more than an individual person could in much less time—picking up trash in their local park, looking after a planter on their street, or running a Neighborhood Watch group—and it's much more fun if you're doing it with others and there's the added promise of a cup of coffee (and some new friends). All of this is so empowering as we realize it's possible for us to make a difference on our own doorsteps, together as a group.

On an individual level, these activities and new friends will extend your support network—maybe someone within walking distance who might be able to lend you a fiver, help look after your kids, have a gossip, make you feel less alone, and vice versa.

Having a support network takes the pressure off too. We can relax in the knowledge that there's no need for us to do it *all* ourselves, no need to be always at our best—the load can be shared. So connecting with groups can also be an act of self-compassion. Within a strong community, if one of us is having a bad day, it's no big deal: the group can support the individual and carry them for a while. If we're having a great day, that's wonderful: all your ideas, inspiration, and energy can be brought to the group.

In my case, being friendly with my neighbors meant I had someone to help me break my back window when I'd locked myself *out* of the house and my dog *in* the house, and enough of my neighbors knew me to not be alarmed or call the police when they saw me smashing in that window with a claw hammer; they knew I had just locked myself out (again). It also meant I had someone to walk my dog when I was ill, to tidy up the garden for me when my unplanned, ahem, "rewilding" got a bit out of hand, and to pick up provisions for me during the coronavirus lockdown when I couldn't go out myself. It helps. I feel safer. I know that if something unexpected, dangerous, or life-threatening happens, I have neighbors to call on who would help me out. They, in turn, know they have me. We can all face bad times with hope, knowing we aren't alone.

If you're not already playing an active part in your community and are unsure how to start building that local support network, there are loads of opportunities out there—from gospel choirs, the Women's Institute, and upcycling schemes to film groups, art projects, and boxing gyms. They'll give you the ideal opportunity to meet new people with similar interests and to try something new for yourself—stimulating the development of new neural pathways in your brain, enabling electric impulses to travel faster across them, keeping your mind strong and agile.

One of the many positives about the resources of this incredible time in which we live is that it is much easier to find yourself a group. Wondering if anyone shares your budding interest in the history of nineteenth-century pipe smokers? You bet they do. Want to join an over-fifties climbing club? Easy. You'd like to walk with other dog owners while chatting about books? Ditto. Want to find a parkour group in your area? It won't take long.

try this:
WHAT DO YOU FANCY?

Ask yourself: What would you like to try, learn, or change? Who would you like to meet? What kind of group or activity might make you feel inspired? You don't have to take action yet. Just think about it. If doubts and fears creep in, let them. It can feel like a risk to connect, to reach out to people, to make yourself vulnerable. No doubt it takes courage, but the rewards of fun and friendship, growth and positivity, of a joyful experience with a group of like-minded people far outweigh all that. Once you have identified something, you can start investigating what is available in your local area.

I've seen firsthand how a shared experience can bring a group of people together, lift everyone's spirits, and, for some, be life changing in the hope it brings.

My friend Emma Waterford is the most wonderful artist. Like me, she believes in joy as a mighty force for good. So when a group of people from a sheltered housing residence expressed a longing to get together and do something fun, we were more than ready to help. Obviously, we settled on cabaret. On our first visit, around eight people from the thirty or so flats joined us in the communal lounge, and we sat down with tea and cookies and started to make plans. There was a bit of awkwardness and shyness at first, but soon people began to open up. Some of them told us that they were lonely or bored and others felt pessimistic about the future, but we also discovered a lot of enthusiasm and hope that we would create something amazing together.

The project was a collective endeavor, not led by Emma and me, but planned together as a group. We learned song and dance routines, made decorations, and devised cabaret names for each member of the troupe inspired by their favorite cookies—such as Kitty Custard Cream. On the day of the party, we transformed the place into a glittering, glamorous, colorful wonderland. Our guests were entertained with stories, jokes, and singalongs. A couple of residents got up with the band to perform solos; everyone tried out our burlesque routine from their seats. An hour and a half in, and up sprang from nowhere a raucous, unruly, improvised bacchanalian spiral dance. One of the residents, laughing her socks off, said to me, "This is a Thursday afternoon in a sheltered housing unit for the over sixties, not a Parisian bordello. Look at us!"

I found myself hoping I'd end up living somewhere like this— such a great community to be part of in later life. We had done this together. We had defeated the many-headed hydra of loneliness, boredom, depression, and despair with fun, joy, our glad rags, and fancy dances.

This whole experience was made possible by a project called Meet Me At, dreamt up in 2013 by David Slater (the artistic director of Entelechy Arts), Gavin Barlow (artistic director of the Albany Arts Center), and members of their local authority. This creative arts club was set up to counter isolation, depression, and anxiety in older people. For those who became a part of this extended network, it was transformative. One of the participants said: "They saved me, brought me back into the world, so I feel now I am part of something really special." This is why local groups and organizations are so important.

As David said to me, "communities create the condition for hope." They are the fertile ground in which hope can grow. Another such organization is the New Note Orchestra, the first of its kind in the UK, made up of people in recovery from addiction. Simply by existing, it sows seeds of hope. Founded by TV producer Molly Mathieson, it shows that it's possible to recover from addiction, and to be part of a compassionate and creative group with a common purpose.

I attended one of their concerts, which included poetry, short films, and animations, and it was joyous, a real hope-booster. After the show, I spoke with Malcolm, a dapper gent who plays the electric guitar. He'd started drinking to cope with his speech impediment, then quickly found he couldn't stop. He told me he'd felt

trapped by the horror of the life I was living, being in and out of prison for years. At one point I was sleeping underneath a bridge, there was water coming down on me, it was terrible and there were these kids shouting, "Get up, you old drunken bum!" and I wanted to say to them, "No! I'm not what you think I am, I can draw, I can play music!" Then I saw my reflection with the wine stains on my top, and I thought: they are right, I am an old drunken bum. I faced my fears and gradually built up my confidence after getting into rehab.

Malcolm immersed himself in music after finding his way to the orchestra, and now he also runs a weekly music workshop in a hostel for homeless people. Malcolm explained that music gives everyone a chance to express painful emotions and experiences in such a way that "the ugly things become beautiful." He said, "I find hope in knowing that change is possible, as I am living proof of that." With a twinkle he told me, "I came out of jail with one crap guitar. Now I have ten and my own studio."

So often, new communities are created when there's a desperate need for something to exist, to fill the gap that nobody else is filling. When local children's services were cut in 2013, Moira Kerrane got a group of mums together, took on a vacant building, and "on a wing and a prayer" they got started with a play club, hoping they'd be able to pay the bills and keep it going. It began with twenty parents, and six years later 650 families have passed through its doors. Now Moira has all sorts of plans for the future, from making the playgroup environmentally friendly to starting a cooking skills workshop.

Moira is a passionate advocate of grassroots action: This is where I find hope, right here. We cannot wait on governments, and we can't take on the whole world. It has to be done locally, and with the support of the local council, we are getting things done, connecting with other local groups, and helping each other.

try this:
INVITATION

Could you create a space for hope to grow? Do you have a skill you could share, or could you invite people in and listen? All you need is a place and some people—it may not seem much but this is a powerful start. It doesn't have to be anything fancy or grand. Why not invite a group for a cup of coffee and see what happens? Don't worry if it's a little bit awkward to begin with; that will soon pass. It might be that a clear collective purpose or common interest emerges once you've created the conditions for the group to exist—and then you can begin to establish your aim in whatever way feels right for your new community. Because that's what you've just created.

Nothing demonstrates the importance of collective action more than a crisis or a tragedy. When something of this nature occurs, it's hard to witness and experience the suffering that goes with it, but seeing people pull together can nevertheless be inspiring, and—as with the recent pandemic—can help create the hope that there is a way to get through it.

On the morning of Wednesday June 14, 2017, I got up at 5 :00 a.m. and checked social media and the TV news to see what was happening in the world. What I saw was horrific—a tower block engulfed in flames.

I volunteered to help coordinate the donations that poured in as people across the country responded to the lives lost and changed forever by that awful fire at Grenfell Tower in West London. Outside Kensington Town Hall, I saw a van unloading a huge amount of bottled water, and people carrying bags and pushing trolleys full of food, clothes, and toys. Everywhere there were piles of donations of all kinds. It was incredible to see such goodwill in the face of such horror.

The council workers had organized lunch for the volunteers, and we all had a chance to talk to each other. It was then that I realized how far people had come to help and what they had sacrificed to do so—taking hours off work and foregoing their pay, staying on friends' sofas, donating their time and energy.

For the next few weeks, there were some incredible stories of what people were doing for Grenfell victims and survivors: Jo Maugham QC offering free legal advice to survivors; Marks & Spencer sending a refrigerated truck to help preserve perishable food donations; local religious groups, businesses, and individuals offering temporary accommodation, money, and food to those affected. We Londoners, accustomed to being told that we're an unfriendly and uncaring bunch, were inspired, proud of our city, encouraged, and humbled by the response.

There is still a lot of grief and anger about Grenfell and the deaths of seventy-two people—and rightly so, especially as many questions remain unanswered about the events of that terrible day. The campaign group Grenfell United, composed of survivors and bereaved families, continue to work for safe homes, justice and change, and it has provided a platform for people to find their voices and to express pain and anger, as well as hopes and plans for the future. The strongest desire is that this never happens again and is never forgotten. Yet I think it's vital we remember how people helped each other. We're often told that people don't care, but the public response to the Grenfell fire, the volunteers and support groups that sprang up afterward to help the bereaved as well as the children and their families who survived, are reminders of how ready we are to help each other. We can allow ourselves to find hope in the essential goodness of human beings, knowing that in the aftermath of tragedies, of natural or human-made disasters, it is not selfishness that usually prevails but generosity and kindness. During the pandemic too, mutual aid groups sprang up all over the world, a huge outpouring of compassion and generosity that we all witnessed, allowing us all to feel more hopeful about getting through these challenging times.

try this:
COME JOIN US

If you or someone you know helps people in any way, whether it be in times of disaster or otherwise, don't be scared to share.

Friends and family will be encouraged when they are told what you or others have done to help. It will give them hope (that we humans can and do look after each other) and hope for themselves (I could do that!). Let people know the problem, who is helping and how. Invite them to join you if they can.

We can find examples of people eagerly pitching in all over the world: donations and assistance given in abundance during bushfires in Australia; Texas citizens donating and delivering boats to survivors of Hurricane Katrina in New Orleans; churches filled with food and clothes for the victims of Storm Desmond in Cumbria; donations collected in scout huts and community centers for the refugee camps in Calais, Scotland, and Greece. During the 2020 coronavirus pandemic, there was the story of Captain Tom Moore, a British veteran who, at the age of ninety-nine, set out alone to raise £1,000 for the NHS by walking one hundred times up and down his garden. His wonderful intention was touched many and became a collective endeavor, with more than £30 million being donated by the public.

In her beautifully hopeful account of human nature, *A Paradise Built in Hell: The Extraordinary Communities That Arise in Disaster*, the writer Rebecca Solnit observed: "In the wake of an earthquake, a bombing, or a major storm, most people are altruistic, urgently engaged in caring for themselves and those around them, strangers and neighbors as well as friends and loved ones."

Connections and community are vital in so many ways, as I hope my stories have demonstrated, from a bit of fun to lifesaving aid. David, from Meet Me At, said:

> I am happy to be one starling in a murmuration. About me there are others, in my peripheral vision, each doing the same. We fly alongside each other, we sometimes meet, we sometimes speak, mostly we just know we are there, getting it wrong now and then; it's beautiful and clumsy. That is hope to me.

I hope you find your stories, of local people and places from the past and present, to inspire you, to give you hope. And when you do, imagine them multiplied many times over in every town and city across this country, across Europe, across the world, groups held together by common purposes, by common interests, by friendship, by love, by hope.

CHAPTER SIX

the edgelands

FINDING THE BALANCE BETWEEN GOOD NEWS AND BAD

....

> "KEEP YOUR FACE ALWAYS TOWARD
> THE SUNSHINE—AND SHADOWS
> WILL FALL BEHIND YOU."
>
> —WALT WHITMAN

I RECENTLY CONDUCTED A STRAW POLL among my friends and contacts by posting this question on Facebook: "Just wondering, do any of you avoid watching the news?" This differed from my usual kind of posts, such as "Has anyone ever actually slipped on a banana skin? Because I just did that" or "Has anyone ever found a stranger's shopping list and if so please share." I didn't necessarily think that my latest offering would get much of a response, being a bit lacking in dramatic visual content and humor. However, to my surprise, the replies came thick and fast. Overwhelmingly the answer was yes.

Most of my friends and contacts were avoiding the news. The reasons weren't surprising but included: it's "too depressing," "I avoid it for my own sanity," it's "dumbed down," "too scary," "biased," "full of lies," there's "too much hate and rage."

Most upsetting for me was a message from my friend Karen Dawson:

> *After Christmas, the lunchtime news on my favorite radio station led on a particularly heartbreaking, tragic story, one of those you can do nothing about but can't stop thinking about for days, sandwiched between jolly alternative Christmas songs. I struggle to stay level most of the time and something like that is all it takes to knock me down for the rest of the day. It's gotten to the point where I've stopped listening to the radio altogether, I've just run out of resilience.*

I believe that many of us are switching off the news, like Karen, because it's making us miserable. Often the messages it delivers are so hopeless that we feel utterly powerless to change anything about the situations on our screens. Is it any wonder? Our daily, hourly, minute-by-minute updates seem to be filled with terrible stories: an aerial shot of a forest on fire in the Blue Mountains National Park in Australia, burnt koalas crawling through blackened tree stumps. An overcrowded dinghy full of desperate, worried people in the Mediterranean. A park full of tents sheltering homeless people in Brighton, England. A camp in Calais, France, full of tents and children playing with sticks. A turtle found in Missouri, USA, caught in a plastic six-pack ring and unable to escape. The shantytowns in

Marsh Harbor, in the Bahamas, reduced to matchsticks by Hurricane Dorian. A woman covered in dust cradling a baby in a bombed-out house in Douma, Syria, people running, a city reduced to ash.

In the face of all of this, I can see how tempting it might be to disengage from the news altogether, to avert our eyes and protect ourselves from the feelings of misery and powerlessness this barrage of sadness and tragedy creates. But perhaps removing ourselves completely from what our fellow humans and the natural world are experiencing isn't the best way to deal with it either. So how do we keep our hope alive, in the face of all of this?

Among the responses to my Facebook post, almost buried by the outpourings of fear, despair, frustration, boredom, and mistrust, there was a reply that stood out to me from my friend Flick:

> I read and listen to the news all the time. It's important to be informed, otherwise we end up in situations like we are now. It doesn't need to make you miserable, in fact it can be incredibly empowering to see where one is in the world and what needs to be done to encourage others to join in with positive action.

I agree that shutting the door on all the sad and bad things out there is unhelpful, because simply ignoring problems doesn't make them go away, and some of them are so enormous (such as the effects of climate change) that there is little doubt they will be impacting our own lives soon. I believe it's better to try to face these challenges with courage and find ways to help make things better where and when we're able. But I also know that not everyone feels motivated to take "positive action" by being constantly surrounded by terrible news: it's frightening, and fear can immobilize us.

Science tells us that we're hardwired to respond to fear, and that this response evolved as a survival mechanism, enabling people and other mammals to react quickly to life-threatening situations: "fight, flight, or freeze." According to psychotherapist Susanne Babbel, constant exposure to fear and trauma puts us into stress mode, with a continuous release of stress hormones like cortisol and adrenaline. Susanne explains how this can lead to adrenal fatigue, which in turn can lead to "being tired in the morning, lack of restful sleep, anxiety, and depression, as well as a multitude of other symptoms." In other words, too much bad news can make us ill. Being in this state is no good for us or for anyone else.

It seems to me that we need to find a way to engage with the news—to gain useful and important information about the world we all live in—but on a level that doesn't overwhelm us and feed into a cycle of pessimism and despair that can feel completely paralyzing. So together, we're going to find a way to get out from under our duvets and nurture our sense of hope.

We need to rebalance our media diet so that it becomes more hope focused, while keeping an eye on the headlines, so we're able to use the news as a source of strength and of ideas for positive action. I'd like to help you reach a compromise between ignoring the news completely and obsessing over it. I'd like us all to find a place between despair (claiming that "the end is nigh" and therefore everything is pointless) and denial (eating ice cream in a meadow, while we ignore the forest fire raging behind us) where creative responses can grow and flourish. I call this place the Edgelands.

In the Edgelands, there is a safe, fertile space where the wildflowers of hope can grow. It's quiet here, but it's a little neglected, and it can be a bit uncomfortable, sitting between those two extremes. The first shoots of possibility spring up here, like daisies popping up in the cracks of the pavement. There is space here for creativity and dreaming, action and learning, for keeping each other company and for encouragement.

First of all, it's important to remember that although there are always terrible things going on in the world, on any given day, there are plenty of positive news stories too. One of the issues with finding them is that mainstream media outlets often focus on more negative news—in part because there has been a belief (sometimes backed up by higher numbers of clicks and shares) that these are the stories people are drawn toward. Perhaps it's our negativity bias at work again, compelling us to read those stories so we can know what might threaten our survival. There is evidence to suggest that these stories attract greater quantities of readers, viewers, and listeners—providing more exposure to advertisers and therefore more advertising income.

Yet these stories aren't the only realities. There is the town of Narberth, in Wales, welcoming refugee families into their community. The remote village of Shikarpur in Bangladesh using solar panels to create and share their own power. An isolated older lady in Sheffield, England, receiving thousands of birthday cards and gifts on the occasion of her one hundredth birthday after her story was shared online, from countries including America, Japan, Australia, New Zealand, and Romania.

try this:
REBALANCING OUR MEDIA DIET

For the next twenty-four hours, pay close attention to the stories you hear and the images you see across all sources: news stories, social media feeds, conversations with friends and family, all of it. Consider their messages. How many of those stories are negative and how many positive?

If you didn't come across any positive ones naturally (and that's always possible in our gloom-laden news agenda), actively look for some: I promise they are out there. Take a conscious break from negative stories to acknowledge that, despite them, there are good things and good people out there.

These positive stories are not often front-page news in the mainstream media, but coming across one of them can sometimes be just what we need to help lift our hope. After the 2019 general election in the UK, I was feeling pretty low, upset, and dismayed by the aggression and hostility expressed in Parliament during the campaign. So I was immensely grateful in the run-up to Christmas that the BBC Breakfast show seemed to be ramping up their feel-good content. One morning when I switched on, they were telling the story of Terrance, seventy-eight, from Oldham in Greater Manchester, who had spent the past twenty-one Christmases alone. His story so touched people that students from Oldham College gifted him a Christmas tree and sang "Silent Night" with him on his doorstep. It was a hopeful, beautiful story of people responding with kindness when they knew this man was in trouble. Age UK reported a massive upsurge in people volunteering for their "befriending" services for the elderly, proof of the immense positive impact that sharing these stories can have. We see someone doing something good, we think we can do it too, then we do it. "Thank you," I half wept, half whispered to the TV. Thank you. There is hope for us all.

During the coronavirus pandemic, there was a big increase in people seeking out hopeful, positive news. In March 2020, actor John Krasinski brought out a "news network for good news" on YouTube; within a week, Some Good News had more than 1.5 million subscribers and 25 million views. Google searches for "good news" spiked in April 2020 and continued to rise. A constant stream of negative news is no longer serving us; far from ensuring our survival, it is threatening it by producing fear and inaction in people, as well as making some of us deeply miserable.

"Good news" can be really beneficial in giving us a break from the onslaught, yet we can't solely focus on these stories. A good-news story in one place doesn't negate the damage done in another, nor the pain that can make us feel. However, there are different types of positive news. There are the plain and simple stories of wonderful things happening in the world (for example the story of a group of teenage boys delivering care packages to isolated older people in their town during lockdown), and there are stories about enormous problems and challenges that also offer up possible solutions (for example the news that honeybees are in steep decline, but with ideas of how to help them by choosing what we plant in our gardens carefully and information about organizations worldwide who are addressing this issue constructively). These stories, in part, become ones of creativity, innovation, and invention that encourage us to act.

It seems this approach has merit. Positive psychology researcher Jodie Jackson conducted a study at the University of East London on the effects of consuming constructive journalism. Her research found that "on an individual level, news stories that focused on solutions were shown to boost self-efficacy; a person's belief in their ability to make a difference." The study also found that these news stories led to an increase in optimism, encouraged people to tackle a problem rather than avoid it, and inspired them to take part in their community and try to make a difference. These are all persuasive reasons for changing how we consume the news.

This "solutions-driven journalism," encouraging a more hope-fueled media landscape, is something that news presenter Martyn Lewis has been promoting since 1993. I first heard Martyn speak when I was invited to an event hosted by my friends at Action for Happiness in Conway Hall, London, back in 2015. It's no exaggeration to say that this single evening changed forever the way I engage with news, and Martyn's talk helped me recover hope when it was waning: "The main criteria for commissioning stories should not be the degree of violence, death, conflict, failure or disaster that they encompass," he said, "but the extent to which those stories shape or change, or have the potential to shape or change, the country or the world in which we live" so that "people are kept fully aware of the changes which offer hope"—even when, at first glance, the main issue might be a negative one. In his talk Martyn spoke about how, while he understands why so many journalists focus on the stories of young people being "rioters, vandals, muggers, or looters," he doesn't understand why there is no parallel reporting of young people serving their communities in positive ways. He cited an example of the young people who set up a community radio station in North Lambeth, with local police reporting that since they went on air, youth crime had stopped completely. Yet, as he said, "not a single national media journalist thought that worth reporting."

Since Martyn Lewis's initial appeal for reconsidering the way news is presented, things have begun to transform for the better. There is an increasing number of constructive and solution-driven stories coming from the establishment media—such as the *New York Times*, *Huffington Post's The Brightside*, and the BBC's World Hacks—but also from websites such as the Good News Network and Kickstarter-funded publications such as the beautifully illustrated *The Happy Newspaper*. This is a move in the right direction, but there is certainly more work to be done.

One organization that really champions this approach is Positive News. Gavin Haines, one of its reporters, explains how they are

> *shining a spotlight on those who are outside the narratives of mainstream media, but who are trying to do good and create positive change in what are quite dark times. The organizations we partner with as advertisers are also trying to do good, so what we are cocreating is an ecosystem of hope.*

It seems they have plenty of material to draw on. "There are loads of switched-on young entrepreneurs doing really interesting things to try to avert the climate crisis, for example," Gavin explained. "Although these times we find ourselves in can seem incredibly bleak, the challenges are forcing people to come up with some brilliant and interesting innovations. There is real positive change happening out there."

I love this idea—that there are people all over the world doing positive things, all part of a network of hope we can connect with, support, and join. Gavin's favorite hopeful story of recent times was a visit to Blue City in Rotterdam.

Blue City is an incubator for circular entrepreneurs—those whose innovations are aimed at eliminating waste and promoting the reuse of resources, as opposed to the more traditional "take, make, and dispose" model of production. Two young entrepreneurs came up with an idea for repurposing used wet wipes. They fish them from the sewers, where they cause big problems with blockage, clean them a little, shred, compress, and dry them, and then cut them into sheets that are used as a growing medium for plants on green roofs—literally a roof made of living plants. The recycled wet wipes are perfect as they have a great ability to retain water and, as Gavin delicately described, "the plants love the tangled mess of wet wipes because they still have—ahem—organic matter in them, and the plants thrive."

This story helps us move away from focusing on how terrible it is that we throw out so many nonbiodegradable wet wipes, gradually spiraling into despair about yet another element of our environmental crisis, to see creative solutions that are happening right now. The problem is acknowledged, but the focus is on how we might fix it, hopefully inspiring us to support these innovations or even to make us consider our own solutions to other seemingly insurmountable problems. We aren't all going to come up with a way to recycle wet wipes, but after hearing this story, Gavin was motivated to plant his own green roof, which has so many environmental benefits, such as providing insulation and creating a habitat for wildlife.

try this:
POSITIVE NEWS

If you would like to engage with positive news and constructive journalism:

1. Subscribe to as many publications as you can, as this will ensure these publications thrive and continue. There are also plenty of resources and newsletters you can sign up to for free—just do what you are able.

2. On social media and the internet, engage with people and organizations who promote constructive journalism and positive news—there are some listed at the end of the book to get you started.

3. Share constructive and hope-filled stories with as many people as you can.

4. If there are people or news sources that provide stories that consistently make you feel hopeless or depressed, consider avoiding them, at least for a while.

5. Read beyond the headlines if something has piqued your curiosity, so you can get a deeper understanding and maybe discover similar or related stories.

The last thing that Gavin said to me was about creating new

hope—what we do once we've read a positive story and feel inspired to do something ourselves: "We can't just read a bit of nice news and say 'That's all going well' and do nothing. We have to be active and we have to do things to make it happen."

If you worry that by focusing more strongly on positive news that I'm being blithely optimistic about the harsh reality of the world, I'd say this: the true reality of the world is complex and includes both good and bad, challenges and opportunities. At the very least, reading positive news and solutions-focused stories will have a beneficial effect on your mental health. Instead of flooding your system with anxiety-inducing cortisol, with only a narrow view of what is going on in the world, you will allow yourself to see a truer, fuller reflection. But even better, when you read these stories of people being creative, innovative, and proactive, you might even join them or support them. We can choose to be part of the changes in our world in a positive way, by hoping and believing that things can and do get better—by taking action.

In 2019, a woman named Libby read an article on social media about a "community store," based in a scout hut in Scotland, which enabled local residents on low incomes to collect good quality surplus supermarket food. All it cost the residents was a small affordable monthly membership fee. Recognizing that this was something very much needed in her local community in South London, Libby set about creating a similar project herself. She found a website dedicated to helping people do just this, and she secured help from the local authority and residents, partnered with a food charity, and liaised with nearby businesses and shops. Within months, they had enough volunteers to open their doors, and by 2020, they had forty members. Libby said, "If I hadn't read that story, I might not have had the confidence to try it myself. It was good to see how other people had done it and see that it is possible to make a real difference to your community."

Reading just one positive news story gave Libby the hope that she had the power to make a difference and moved her to take action of her own.

try this:
GOOD NEWS ROUND-UP

At the end of every week, I do a brief roundup of all the positive news I encountered and consider how I can support it or take inspiration from it. It's especially important if the week has been a tough one as it helps to restore my hope and carry me forward. Here are a few examples so you can try your own version of this.

Environmental campaigners in Kenya build a boat out of old flip-flops to raise awareness about plastic in the oceans.

Action: Cut down on use of plastic bags.

Germany is turning sixty-two military bases into wildlife sanctuaries.

Action: Visit a local wildlife sanctuary and support them with your entrance fee or a donation. Or if you have a garden, try a rewilding project of your own.

The world is 5 percent greener now than it was two decades ago, according to NASA.

Action: Plant a tree.

In so many ways, we live in a time of great wonders. Those of us lucky enough to have smartphones are carrying around in our back pockets a device that can access much of the knowledge of humanity. Given its enormous potential, it seems a shame to waste it on arguing with strangers over politics or reading anger-filled comment threads that keep us up at night worrying. Let's use all the tools at our disposal for good instead, as part of that "ecosystem of hope" described by Gavin. Chat to your neighbors, friends, parents, and children about the stories you've discovered while exploring constructive journalism. Enjoy the telling and notice how people respond. Share these positive actions on social media, get their message out there. Who knows who might be inspired by them? At the very least, you're helping to break the endless feedback loop of negativity, anxiety, and fear that we so often find ourselves reacting and contributing to through our interactions on social media. Instead, you'll be spreading a bit more hope across the world.

There may well be times, however—even if we've been buoying ourselves up with solutions-focused media—that we might need a bit of a break from it all. The way we consume news has changed in the twenty-first century. We no longer simply read the newspapers in the morning or catch up with the TV report in the evening. We have access to instantly responsive, twenty-four-hour rolling news, seeing events happen in real time. In some ways, this is incredibly useful, but it can also be relentless and draining, particularly when there are a lot of big news stories happening all at once. In recent years, we've been bombarded with divisive elections, the environmental crisis, coronavirus...

A total news blackout wouldn't be appropriate nor sustainable for many of us long-term, but if your mental health is suffering, if you're feeling overwhelmed by grief or anxiety, do not feel in the least bit guilty about giving yourself some space. Step away from your devices, turn off the radio and television news, log out of social media, and allow yourself to recalibrate. It's very difficult to take action, to feel hopeful, if you're having this negative experience. Once you feel ready to reengage with the news, use the checklist below to help you connect in a more positive way. I've found these immensely helpful.

try this:
SWITCH OFF

1. Decide a daily time limit for engaging with the news and try to be strict with yourself on this. Be especially mindful of time when online. It's so easy to get sucked into that vortex of negative stories that fuel your panic without offering any possible solutions.

2. Look at the news at the same time every day for the same length of time.

3. Don't get drawn into obsessively following breaking news bulletins of key events. You're unlikely to learn anything new by constantly refreshing the feed and it may make you more anxious. Check in a few times if you feel you have to, but disengage in between and do something else.

4. If a particular piece of news really knocks you, try to consider if there is a positive angle or a possible solution. There will always be someone, somewhere, with ideas of how to respond positively or news of a potential way forward. Use positive words or phrases in your search engine, such as "how can we help?" or "what are the solutions to...?" or "organizations helping with..." This may help you connect with even

more interesting projects or publications, adding to your library of positive news sources.

I began this chapter with my Facebook straw poll and all those friends and acquaintances who have stepped away from the news because engaging with it was too painful, disempowering, and depressing for them. But I don't believe it has to be this way. By exploring a different approach to experiencing the news, we can use it as a source of hope and a call to action. We can consider those stories and say to ourselves: that thing that floored you, that shook your resilience, that made you feel such pain or fear...here is something you can do that helps, that changes that picture, that changes that story, that creates hope. Hope is not the same as denial, nor does it require denial, but it does need protecting and nurturing. By reassessing how we engage with the news, we can find ways to stay informed without giving in to despair. We can find a way to settle in those Edgelands, to imagine how else things might be, and then— alongside those who sit with us—to act with hope, creating hope, helping change happen.

CHAPTER SEVEN
deeds and words

TAKING POSITIVE ACTION

....

**"IF YOU DON'T LIKE THE NEWS, GO OUT
AND MAKE SOME OF YOUR OWN."**

—WES NISKER

I N 2014, ARTIST ROB KENNEDY and I began a project called Sign of the Times. We were interested in the history of protests and placards (and if any of you have been to or seen footage of a march recently, you may have noticed how witty, creative, and powerful the signs can be). We thought about the history of protests and how often they are led by a negative message—"we are against..." or "we want to stop..."—and considered instead the impact of declaring what it is we *do* want.

In the foyers of local arts and community centers, we asked people to think about the things they wanted and to write down ten of them. Anything was allowed, as long as it wasn't unkind or aggressive—and today, having delivered this workshop many times by now, it's worth mentioning that the answers have never been either. Because ten is quite a lot of "wants," it encouraged participants (including ourselves) to get past the obvious and discover something surprising. The answers were sometimes as light-hearted as "I want more time to dance," as personal as "I want my dad to accept me," or about larger world issues such as "an end to systemic racism."

The second part of the process was getting people to choose which item on the list they felt was most important to them and to make a placard with those chosen words emblazoned across it.

In Swansea, we all marched with our placards, with our chants of hope ringing down the high street: "What do we want? More kindness! When do we want it? Now! What do we want? Everyone to laugh more! When do we want it? Now!" Afterward, we attached the placards to the railings outside an abandoned theater. Many people stopped to look and ask questions, and interesting conversations sprang up between complete strangers. It was playful, funny, and thought-provoking. It showed us what we had in common, with many expressions of hope for a fairer, kinder world. It felt like it allowed the *possibility* of positive change, by giving space to these expressions of hope. After all, if we can't imagine what we want, how can we then create it or try to make it happen? Action depends upon our ability to conjure up something different in our minds.

As we've discovered, taking action is a key part of our landscape of hope. There's no doubt, however, that taking action on a larger scale can be a daunting prospect. It's not always clear how to go about it—or even which cause to offer your time and energies to. So that's exactly what this chapter is going to consider.

---

try this:
TOP TEN

Give yourself time and space to answer this open question: What do you want? Write a list of ten. You can do this alone, with a partner, or in a group. Remember, we're looking for a "want," not a "don't want" (we had to remind ourselves of this often during Sign of the Times). For example, if one of your wants is "I don't want to struggle to get on the bus," you could rephrase that as "I want better access everywhere for wheelchair users like me." For now, use this exercise as a way of exploring what's important to you. All your wants are valid. We'll come back to them later and consider what actions we could take to bring these wants closer.

In order to think about the connections between our hopes for ourselves and the wider world, and how those hopes might be made a reality, we're going to explore some really successful campaigns, to hear the stories of how they moved from thoughts to words to deeds, and to ask what happened next.

As part of Sign of the Times, we created a slideshow of images from 1903 to the present day showing placards, protests, demonstrations, and marches from all over the world. It was very powerful to see that throughout history, we humans have been striving for positive change.

One of the first images I found was of a smiling woman in a smart hat and a tweed jacket holding up a large sign that simply said "Votes for Women." This campaign always speaks to me. Without the actions of these women, I wouldn't have the right vote, to participate in politics on an equal legal footing with men. I realized, however, that I wanted to know more about the original protestors and how they were driven to act. Suzanne Keyte also feels that there is much to be learned from how these women took their wants or hopes and turned them into action—and got results. She began her career at the Women's Library and was "blown away" by what she found: the largest collection of suffragette and suffragist material in the world. "It is so important that we know what has been achieved," she told me. "These are inspiring stories that aren't told or shared as often as they should be."

Since the 1860s, the law-abiding suffragists, led by Millicent Fawcett, had been campaigning for the right for women to vote. These women wanted votes for themselves as individuals of course, but they extended their hopes to all women. In 1903, frustrated by the lack of progress in the suffragist campaign, a group of women gathered with Emmeline Pankhurst and her daughters at their home in Manchester. They settled on one aim, "Votes for Women" under one motto: "Deeds Not Words." They were soon given the nickname "suffragettes" by the *Daily Mail*. Intended as a slur, the name was happily adopted by the new group.

The suffragettes began to adopt increasingly unlawful and disruptive methods to achieve their aims, and many of the women suffered greatly through humiliation, ridicule, arrest, and hunger strikes. On November 18, 1910, known as Black Friday, a demonstration in Trafalgar Square led to the women being set upon by the police. Two of them died. Nevertheless, thanks to their determination and perseverance, in 1918, the first women in the UK were allowed to vote—though it would be another ten years before all women received the vote on the same terms as men.

I asked Suzanne if there were lessons here that we could apply to our own hopes for positive change, our own campaigns, however big or small. She said:

> It's true that we are in different times now, but what we can learn is that women underestimate themselves, and history underestimates women too, but when they come together and campaign, it can be an amazing thing.

Looking back at something that led to a huge and positive change is a brilliant way to find encouragement for our own efforts. When we can see how others have gone about achieving the seemingly impossible, it shows us the power of a strong notion of a different way forward, that opening up of change and potential.

---

try this:
THE ANCESTORS

Think about a change in history that benefits you today. It could be free education, healthcare, your human and civil rights, an invention, or a scientific advance.

Once you've decided, focus on one aspect of that change and find one person who contributed in some way, great or small. Hold that person gently in your mind and thank them for what they did. You could write them a thank-you letter, keeping it safe for when your hope is waning, so you may be reminded of the difference that an individual's actions can make to so many lives.

As the suffragettes' campaign showed, taking action to make change happen isn't always easy—to hold on to your hopes and act in the belief of their possibility can be an immense act of courage in itself. However, something else that countless campaigns have shown us is the power of a group of people acting together. Whatever your want—your hope—you don't have to go it alone.

In 2012, Lucy-Anne Holmes and her friends ran a campaign in their pajamas to put a stop to *The Sun* placing naked models on page three of their newspaper. Lucy told me how it all started:

I began by writing a letter to the editor of The Sun, *then I asked myself, this won't be enough, what else can I do? I was literally waking in the night thinking about it, and I thought can I really be the only one? Or can it be that there are loads of us feeling this?*

Of course, Lucy soon discovered that many other people were also dismayed by this daily objectification. Together they continued writing letters as well as using social media to challenge the editorial choices of the paper. By March of the same year, their petition had gathered more than 215,000 signatures, as well as the support of over 140 MPs. Eventually, in 2015, a topless page three became history.

Lucy's campaign was not an easy one—she had to take on a very powerful media organization over several years—but she never gave up. I asked Lucy what advice she would give to someone wanting to start their own campaign.

First of all, I'd say absolutely do it—put all your passion and your creativity into it, and remember to have a good time while you are doing it. Find your buddies, as the highs will be much better with them and the lows you can weather together. It made so much difference to me, creating and being part of a team.

It was not only the community around Lucy that drove her on but also the connection she felt to those in whose footsteps she followed. She told me how she got through the darkest days by taking comfort from history:

I felt as though the women who had gone before were urging us on... that there's a baton that has been passed and it's ours now. It might be that we pass this on to another campaign that comes up. So, you are really connected to people who come before you.

As Lucy discovered, teamwork really is key. Yet we love stories that have a hero. Mahatma Gandhi, Martin Luther King Jr., Nelson Mandela, Mother Teresa, Malala Yousafzai: they are all great people who, with powerful words, great courage, and actions, changed the world. Sometimes it's helpful for a campaign to have a figurehead or key spokesperson, but truthfully, most great things are not done by one person alone. Alongside every "hero" finding ways to change the world is a community of people making those achievements possible. I don't wish to diminish the accomplishments of any individual, but I do wish to champion the collective—and that collective may well be much closer than you'd think.

In July 2018, Kathleen Towler looked out of her window, as she did every day, at the patch of ancient woodland near her house. There had been rumors for a couple of years that they were going to build on the woods, so she had been keeping an eye on developments.

Kathleen realized that the loss of these woods would alter how she lived: "You don't realize how important they are to you until they are threatened."

At the beginning of the campaign to keep this forested area, some individuals had written objections to it being compromised but were being ignored. So Kathleen wrote a letter that was signed by many different local organizations and presented it publicly at a council meeting so they could no longer be pushed aside. This joint letter was turned into an online petition and residents went door-to-door gathering signatures. They then gained support from the local press and from the London Wildlife Trust, who manage the wood. Eventually, the campaign had the names of 855 local people all wanting to "preserve and protect these irreplaceable natural assets for the benefit of current and future generations." On Tuesday, October 9, 2018, the council responded by withdrawing the planning application for the proposed housing development. The ancient woodland was saved.

I asked Kathleen what her advice would be for someone wanting to start a local campaign of their own:

You just do whatever you have the energy to do, but you have to realize that you can't do everything. Different people can offer different skills and solutions, so link up with whoever you can and listen to their ideas. Community action is about getting people together, it is more effective as you can't be ignored, and it is not as lonely.

Kathleen now makes sure she enjoys the fruits of their collective endeavor: "Immediately after the campaign I got a dog, so I see much more of the woods now. I appreciate them even more. You hear tawny owls hooting at night. It's lovely." These campaigns on very different scales—from local residents protecting nature to women working for years to change the law of the land—show us that often hope does not lie in the lone hero, but in the potential we have to achieve great things *together*. We saw this more recently too, with the passionate and inspiring global Black Lives Matter protests. All kinds of different people came together and, although there is still a lot of work to be done, there were also many positive results, including police reform, the removal of racist relics, antiracist education reforms, and support for the movement from the sports and entertainment communities. When you allow yourself to acknowledge that you don't have to do it all alone, it can be a huge relief. Or, as the American cultural anthropologist Margaret Mead said: "Never doubt that a small group of thoughtful, committed citizens can change the world; indeed, it's the only thing that ever has."

try this:
THIS IS WHAT I WANT

Earlier in this chapter, I asked you to consider the question "What do you want?" and to compile a list of ten things.

Revisit the list and see if any of them could turn into a campaign or a personal project. Do any of these wants make you feel so strongly that you think you'd like to act on them? Perhaps you already know other people who feel the same way as you, or people who may be able to help you realize your dreams. Connect with groups or organizations whose hopes seem to chime with yours and see what actions they're taking and whether you might be able to join in. Alternatively, start your own group by reaching out and seeing who might like to join you and contribute their time and ideas. Use the internet, social media, and your existing contacts to make a start. Local noticeboards, whether online or offline, can be really effective for issues in your area.

There are many different ways to take action—and they can be effective in very different ways. You don't necessarily have to smash windows to get attention. Sarah Corbett, for example, is the founder of Craftivist Collective, a social enterprise that combines crafts and activism in a unique methodology called "gentle protest."

Sarah was inspired to change tactics after questioning whether her current actions were making a difference. Exhausted by a demanding job on top of her campaigning, she picked up a cross-stitch kit on a long train journey. As she began cross-stitching the teddy in the kit, she noticed the slowness and repetitiveness of the activity was calming her, but it was also catching people's attention. "I was sitting opposite this couple who were asking me what I was doing and I thought, oh my word, crafting is intriguing people. I thought if only I were cross-stitching a quote by Gandhi, we could talk about that."

By the end of the journey, Sarah had decided on her first project: Mini Protest Banners, which she hung in places relevant to particular issues in order to promote thought and action from passers-by in a non-threatening, non-aggressive way. She shared them on social media and set up a blog. It soon became apparent that handicrafts could be very useful indeed—"not to replace other forms of activism but to reach people in an intriguing way." The Craftivist Collective's Marks & Spencer's campaign in 2015 was a beautiful example of this, with the aim of encouraging the company to become a "living wage" employer.

Sarah recruited twenty-four craftivists (male and female) from all over the UK and asked them to embroider an M&S handkerchief and send it to a board member or another influential individual within the company. She asked them to find out what they could about that person so that they could personalize their handkerchief. For example, one board member was a trustee of Kew Gardens, so his handkerchief was covered in flowers and a message about how he could help others flourish. Each handkerchief was intended as a gift, beautifully decorated and accompanied by a handwritten letter filled with hopeful messages, encouraging the person to use their influence to create positive change. And they were very impactful when hand delivered at the M&S AGM, provoking great discussion since everyone wanted to see one another's designs and messages.

In May 2016, Marks & Spencer's made an announcement. They were committing to pay rates above the living wage, leading to fifty thousand employees receiving an increase in salary. The chair of the board told Sarah directly that it was the "most powerful campaign they had ever experienced" and that each time they met they kept talking about the living wage proposal, specifically because of the memorably emotive "gentle protest."

The Craftivist Collective now have a neuroscientist in residence, Dr. Charlotte Rae, who introduced Sarah to the terms "good surprises" and "bad surprises" specifically in relation to activism. Bad surprises might be someone screaming at people through a megaphone. Even if we agree with the message that's being shouted at us, we go into "fight, flight, or freeze" mode, during which we can't listen because our brains are focused on survival, which doesn't help the cause. However, if you give someone a positive interruption—like a beautifully embroidered bespoke handkerchief, perhaps—that's a "good surprise" and will produce dopamine in the brain of the recipient, creating a positive association with you and your message. The discoveries of neuroscience are confirming the powerful effectiveness of "gentle protest." Things can and do change when we find ways to bring people on board to work together to make it happen.

try this:
QUESTIONS AND ANSWERS

As Sarah's campaigning shows, there are many different ways of taking action and many tools at your disposal. She suggested that you might try the following exercise to help you figure out what suits you best.

What is the societal injustice you're concerned about?

What is the solution you want to see? If it was created, how does that solution look, feel, sound, smell, or even taste?

Who has the power to be part of that solution, what kind of power do they hold, and when do they have the power to make decisions or take action to help reach the solution?

Who influences them? It might be that they're not currently influenced by you, but by your neighbor, a customer, the media, or someone else, and that your role is behind the scenes.

What is realistic to ask them to do? Are you asking to change a law? A policy? A behavior? A culture? Or is it a change in their own habits? Or is it a mind shift?

Once you know the goal you want to reach (also knowing that you might never fully reach that utopia), and you know who has the power to be a part of reaching that goal and how, then you can see what skills, influence, and capacity you might be able to offer to be a part of that social change you want to see.

We need to hold on tightly to the hope that we can make a difference, even if we can't take part in a conventional way. Hope is what drives us to continue our fight; without it, when seemingly insurmountable challenges arise, it's tempting to despair and simply give up. In the face of such challenges, we must remember that anything you can do is better than doing nothing. We need to identify what agency and power we each have to change things. We need to know who is already doing what and how we can join or support them. We need hope and workable calls to action, fit for all. So that those who are able to take a week off work to join protestors camping out can do that and have our gratitude and support. And those who can donate to or volunteer at a food bank or spare an hour once a month to share their skills at their local youth club can have our gratitude and support. And those who can help to cheer the others on but don't have the facility for more than that get our gratitude and support too.

try this:
SMALL STEPS

If all this talk of campaigning is feeling overwhelming, there is always something we can do to work toward what we want and to make a positive and hope-filled change in the world. See this as the very beginning of thinking about exactly how you can achieve the changes you would like to see. Here are a few ideas for quick actions that you can do alone with no extra cost and not too much time. And when you're contacting people remember to be gentle and respectful. Try thinking the best of them.

Hope: To see an increase in the use of renewable energy such as wind and solar.

Action: Switch banks and stop giving your money to those who are investing in fossil fuel extraction. Email or write to your bank to let them know why you're leaving them. Move your pension pot, if you have one, to a fund that has divested from fossil fuels, and switch to a green energy supplier. There are useful tips in the chapter notes at the back of the book.

Hope: To see homeless people receive more practical help.

Action: Make a care package for a homeless person from stuff you already have in your house—good things are toiletries, socks, and cereal bars. Email your local government officials and say homeless people in your area really need their help and ask them to do whatever is in their power.

Hope: To live in a world where racism no longer exists.

Action: Be proactive about educating yourself—gain different perspectives by reading authors of races or ethnicities other than your own. Stand against racism in your community by joining a group advocating for the rights of racial or other minorities and volunteer to help if you are able.

These small actions may lead you on to connect with organizations, groups, and like-minded people, and you might even grow your small actions into larger campaigns with the people you find on your journey. It may be that these small actions are enough for you for now, and that's okay too. You'll feel more hopeful about the possibility of positive change once you make a start and see what you are capable of doing, with small steps.

For me, one of the most encouraging things of recent years has been seeing how young people are becoming increasingly galvanized. Throughout history, there have always been children and young people who chose active hope, disrupted "business as usual," and made things hard for us adults in a good way. In 1960, four teenagers refused to leave a lunch counter in Greensboro, North Carolina, at a time when segregation in public spaces still existed, leading to wider lunch counter sit-ins. These protests contributed to the passage of the Civil Rights Act of 1964, outlawing public segregation. On June 16, 1976, a global movement was set in motion against apartheid in South Africa after several thousand students on a peaceful march near Johannesburg were attacked by police with guns and tear gas. And in Prague, a student-led uprising that began on November 17, 1989 grew until the city filled with 500,000 protesters—after eleven days of protest, the Communist Party relinquished power. Today, in protests and conferences viewed and attended by millions across the globe, young people are taking up the mantle, asking adults to take dramatic action and stand with them as they do so.

In 2020, onstage at the World Economic Forum in Davos, Greta Thunberg—who we'll come back to in the next chapter—was on a panel with the title "Forging a Sustainable Path toward a Common Future." Alongside her were three amazingly effective and passionate campaigners: eighteen-year-old Natasha Mwansa, a child and women's rights advocate from Zambia; fifteen-year-old Autumn Peltier, a member of the Wikwemikong First Nation from Ontario,

Canada, and advocate for clean water; and seventeen-year-old Salvador Gómez-Colón, who founded the "Light and Hope" campaign in his home country, Puerto Rico, in the aftermath of Hurricane Maria, raising funds and delivering solar-powered lamps and hand-powered washing machines to the communities on his island. Each of these young panelists spoke powerfully and passionately about their causes, but a strong message stood out from them all: they want us to listen, to really listen, and they want our deeds, not empty words.

Autumn: "If you are going to award me, you can award me by helping me find solutions, award me by helping me to make change... What I want to see is more people trying to help us with what we are trying to achieve."

Salvador: "We've seen our generation standing up for the world... we're not waiting five, ten, twenty years to take the action. We are not the future of the world. We are the present. We are acting now, we are not waiting any longer."

Natasha: "We have powerful voices and powerful minds, and put together, we can foster this powerful energy that can transform society... I am very optimistic about the change we are going to bring... I believe with such powerful minds, who wouldn't have hope?"

With such passionate and energetic young people in the world, we can all look forward to a brighter future with hope. However, instead of leaving them to it, perhaps we might ask ourselves how we can support them and their work. What might we bring to the collective table—large or small? It's up to each of us to find our role, our place in that chain of active hope that leads to change.

try this:
CONNECT WITH A CHILD

This could be your own children or grandchildren, children you care for or teach, the kids of your friends or neighbors. Ask them what their hopes are for the future and what changes they might like to see. It's very encouraging for us adults to listen to the hopes of children and be reminded of their courage and idealism.

Next, help them to investigate that hope further by finding some innovations or inventions in the present that might be moving in that direction or addressing the problem right now. For example, if they would like children all over the world to be safe and looked after, let them know about the UN's Convention on the Rights of the Child so they can see how UNICEF is working to help make sure that those aims are extended worldwide. Find out how they might be able to join in—by subscribing to

> a newsletter or joining a group—and you may want to join in too! Use these resources to investigate what actions could be taken to help them realize the changes they would like to see in the world.

As we've been exploring, there are so many ways for all of us, old and young, to get involved in campaigns that have active hope at their heart. But what about our governments, our elected officials? These are the people who are supposed to be getting things done on our behalf. I know it's easy to become disillusioned with politics. Between the lies and lobbying, party divisions and seeming lack of action, it can sometimes feel as though our politicians aren't always working in our best interests, taking heed of what we have to say or as if we can rely on them to get things done at the right time and in the right way. Thankfully, we do have examples out there of a different kind of politics where deeds, and not only words, matter.

Jacinda Ardern's name comes up a lot in relation to progressive politics. She became New Zealand's youngest prime minister in 2017 and has become an emblem of hope for many people around the world who are yearning for something different, more positive, more compassionate. She gave birth in office, taking her baby to the United Nations and quickly getting the attention of the whole world. In the aftermath of the bombing of mosques in Christchurch, the prime minister was seen hugging the survivors and the families of the victims, wearing a hijab. During the coronavirus crisis, it was widely agreed that her response was a masterclass in leadership. By directing New Zealanders early on to "stay home and save lives," she provided timely meaning and purpose to what people were being asked to do. She also expressed empathy and understanding for people's suffering and gave extensive time for questions from the media in her daily briefings, helping people to make sense of exactly what was happening and why.

In her speech at the General Assembly of the United Nations in 2019, Ardern said:

> *What if we no longer see ourselves based on what we look like, what religion we practice, or where we live? But by what we value. Humanity. Kindness. An innate sense of our connection to each other. And a belief that we are guardians, not just of our home and our planet, but of each other. We are borderless, but we can be connected. We are inherently different, but we have more that we share.*

Hope is a choice we can all make, an act of courage and of caring which we can all achieve. It helps to know that there are leaders in the world right now who stand with us as we dare to make that choice.

Jacinda Ardern is not alone in being a different kind of politician. In Ethiopia, Prime Minister Abiy Ahmed Ali was awarded the 2019 Nobel Peace Prize "for his decisive initiative to resolve the border conflict with neighboring Eritrea." José Mujica, the recent president of Uruguay, was described as "the world's humblest head of state" after he donated around 90 percent of his $12,000 monthly salary to poor people and small entrepreneurs. In September 2013, when he addressed the United Nations General Assembly, he spoke of his urge to return to a simpler way of life focusing on human relationships, love, friendship, adventure, solidarity, and family. Around the world, there are many more politicians and public servants who give us hope through their actions. If we wish to maintain hope in democracy today, it's important for us to acknowledge that politicians are not all the same. There are many who use the keys they hold with great care.

try this: APPEAL

If you think there's action to be taken in your area, write an appeal to your local representative. You might want them to sign a motion, present a question in council meetings, or bring an issue to the attention of the relevant representative.

If you don't already know, find out who your local representatives are and the best way to contact them, whether by post, email, or in person. Start by thanking them for their work and then ask them if they can help.

Even if you're appealing to them about a national or global issue, such as child poverty, make sure your query is personal and local, letting them know how it affects you and you neighborhood specifically, that this is an issue that many people in the area care deeply about.

It'll help if you do some research in advance: find out about your representative's voting record and which political party they're from. This can be pleasantly surprising; politicians who we think might disagree with us sometimes don't. Try to find at least one thing you feel they did well or a vote you agreed with and tell them. This makes a positive and friendly connection from which to build up to your request. Tell them what it is you hope for and why, let them know that their previous good work makes you hopeful that they will support you in this request and might even share your vision. If you've heard nothing back after a few weeks, be sure to follow up politely.

Today, there are moves not only to change the way that individual politicians approach their role, but to change the nature of politics itself, promoting a more hopeful agenda. In October 2018, Lord Dubs, the Labor peer who fled the Nazis in Czechoslovakia as a child, launched Compassion in Politics. This cross-party organization seeks to challenge "the oppressive narrative that says that all humans are just greedy and selfish, and our political system and society must be built in that image."

Co-founders Matt Hawkins and Jennifer Nadel told me: "We were moved to set up Compassion in Politics because we felt there was an urgent need to campaign for and restore a set of values—built on decency, kindness, and inclusion—to our politics."

Its members are working toward introducing a "compassion threshold" into UK policymaking, ensuring that future policies protect the most vulnerable in society and future generations, bringing social justice and environmental justice together. They are also working with lawyers to create a new bill that would extend laws about truth telling within the political world to cover online campaigning and to strengthen the legal consequences of politicians lying in the media or on leaflets and posters. At a grassroots level, there is also a proposal for a new code of conduct to "stop the nastiness." This online petition was created by Lisa, Jaiden, Olivia, and Precious, four young people in Salford and Manchester who "think politicians should be people we can look up to and be inspired by." They are asking the Speaker of the House of Commons to introduce this as soon as possible.

We need to support these attempts, and others, to change the culture of our politics in our regions, countries, and beyond. Doing so will help put the onus on those in power to tell the truth, to act fairly and with compassion. It will also enable young people to look forward to the future with hope and help ensure that the world they inherit will be full of beauty and possibility. We also need young people to be encouraged to get involved in campaigning or politics themselves without fear of being bullied and intimidated. We need to show them that politicians can behave with integrity and honor, and that politicians and political systems can serve the common good.

We must not lower our expectations of our leaders. We must not resign ourselves to lies, misinformation, and bad behavior. We must thank those who are doing their best and gently ask for more from those in power. We should work toward replacing those who cannot or will not listen to the suffering and anguish of the world and its inhabitants. We do this by supporting those who are doing good, by asking more of those who are not doing enough, by challenging those who could do better, and by democratically replacing those who continue to fail us. We do this by lobbying, campaigning, signing petitions, marching, and by taking part in peaceful protests, with witty placards or otherwise.

We can shore up our hope for positive change by remembering the successes of the past and by engaging in campaigns in the present. This way we can all take a role in making change happen, using our deeds—that most active form of hope—as well as our words.

CHAPTER EIGHT

hope is a forest

JOINING THE FIGHT FOR NATURE— AND FOR US ALL

....

> "ONE TOUCH OF NATURE MAKES
> THE WHOLE WORLD KIN."
>
> —WILLIAM SHAKESPEARE

SWEDISH ENVIRONMENTAL ACTIVIST GRETA THUNBERG began learning about climate and environmental breakdown when she was eight years old. In the classroom, she was shown images of plastic in the oceans, starving polar bears, and extreme weather events affecting people across the world. Unable to get the pictures out of her head, by age eleven, she was so depressed she stopped eating and going to school. She was baffled by the seeming lack of action from those in power—the world was in danger, so why wasn't anyone doing anything about it?

Eventually, Greta decided to do something herself. In August 2018, when she was fifteen years old, she sat outside the Swedish Parliament buildings with a handmade sign on which was written

"School Strike for the Climate." She continued to strike every Friday—demanding action—and was soon joined by others. After a couple of weeks, with the help of some press coverage, several more strikes sprang up in towns and cities across Sweden, quickly organizing into a new movement under the name Fridays for Future, which, from there, spread across the world.

Greta has become an inspiring figurehead in the fight for action in this human-caused climate emergency. In 2019, she addressed global leaders at the World Economic Forum in Davos. Her brave, moving, and heartfelt speech reflected her understandable horror at the devastating consequences of global heating on wildlife, people, and the planetary systems on which we *all* depend for our food, water, and a stable climate: "I don't want you to be hopeful. I want you to panic. I want you to feel the fear I feel every day... I want you to act as if the house is on fire, because it is."

There's no doubt the climate emergency is one of the biggest issues humanity faces today. Terrifying information abounds about what our use of fossil fuels is doing to our planet, increasing the risks of drought, flood, extreme heat, ice-melt, sea-level rise, grinding poverty, and hunger for millions of people. This isn't something that's happening elsewhere, affecting others. It's happening to each of us right now and will shape the lives of our children and grandchildren in ways that at times can feel really frightening and difficult to comprehend. Scientists agree that if we want to avoid the most catastrophic effects of global heating on every one of us, carbon emissions must halve by 2030.

I understand what Greta meant when she asked us to panic, when she said she didn't want us to be hopeful—it was a call to urgent action, and she's right to make that call. But to be motivated to take action, I believe we *need* hope: we have to believe that there's a chance that our actions will make a difference. If we're terrified, the danger is we will freeze, give in to our fear, or retreat into denial and do nothing—and that's the last thing we need. On the other hand, hope without action—which is what I believe Greta was really referring to—will do very little to help us either. So what can we do that will make a difference?

As my friend Kate said to me, "It isn't that I don't care. It is that I don't know what to do. The things I can do, like recycling, they just don't seem enough. It almost doesn't seem worth it. It's too much." I agree; it can feel so overwhelming. But there are things we can and must do. The world's wealthiest countries are largely to blame for global climate change and yet it's the poorest countries, and their people, that are already suffering worst. So we citizens of those wealthy countries need nothing less than a revolution in the way we travel, eat, work, consume, shop, in all aspects of our lives, as we spew carbon from our homes, our factories, and our vehicles. It's clear that we need to make permanent changes that have the greatest chance of spreading widely and that will be maintained.

I think a good starting point is to focus on those changes that will also improve our lives, increase our happiness, and give us more joy. If we do this, others will see what's happening, and they'll join us. Doing good and being happy can coexist: indeed, for real, lasting change to happen, it's essential that they do.

try this:
BE THE CHANGE, DO WHAT YOU LOVE

In 2012, I attended a workshop at the School of Life with John-Paul Flintoff called How to Change the World. He spoke brilliantly about avoiding burnout by finding a way to enjoy yourself when working for a cause, as it massively increases your chances of being able to keep it up. Here are a few ideas of how to do that when approaching our climate crisis—small changes in our everyday lives that we can all make and enjoy.

Food: Have a bit of fun changing your diet—use it as a chance to experiment with meat- and dairy-free alternatives, or create something with leftovers (throw a leftovers dinner party, where all guests bring a dish!). Try growing herbs and vegetables and experience the joy of cooking with ingredients you've grown yourself.

Travel: If you're trying to walk or cycle more, find the route that will give you the most pleasure—perhaps the least stressful or most beautiful. Take the time to appreciate your journey and mix it up every now and then so you don't get bored. Share journey tips with friends and family—the best way to persuade other people to walk and cycle more is by showing them how great it can be!

Shop: Sharing, making, fixing, upcycling, repurposing can all be immensely fun and creative, and transform "junk" into lovely homemade gifts. There are lots of YouTube tutorials and free online course that will take you through the basics of making clothes, carpentry, knitting, and ideas for repurposing things that you may otherwise throw away. Get creative and enjoy the beauty of "make do and mend."

Small actions have a multitude of benefits, but of course we know that cycling, eating a few vegan dinners, and buying less can't fix things overnight, and the future can still look sickeningly scary. When something frightening is happening, we tend only to imagine the worst possible outcomes. Climate psychology therapist Caroline Hickman notes how "to deal with that loss of control, we project into the future, sometimes into apocalyptic thinking." As philosopher Edgar Morin says, "life is an ocean of uncertainties"; I find some comfort in that. It can be very helpful to remember that there are many potential outcomes and futures branching out from every moment and every situation, and many of them contain hope and joy. The future is not yet written, and we have the power to shape it both individually and collectively.

It helps to look forward to the future with hope. We still have time to stop the very worst effects of global heating if we act now. We've already seen that it's possible to make a dramatic difference in a very short amount of time: as the world adapted to unprecedented societal change during the coronavirus pandemic, entire countries were shut down overnight. Many places soon noted the effects on the environment, with cleaner air and less pollution. In Jalandhar, India, residents reported being able to see the Himalayas for the first time in almost thirty years. In the "great pause" created by the pandemic, we saw what we had done, what we missed, what we loved and needed, and what might be possible. The world acted as one—imperfectly, yes, but with a single aim: to save lives. We've done it once. Surely we can do it again to save the planet? Of course, the lockdown forced very abrupt changes that would be tricky to sustain, but with a managed transition from harmful systems and practices to sustainable ones, social justice and climate justice can coexist. People and communities would be able to adapt and be supported while the necessary changes take place, for example retraining workers in traditional energy-producing regions so that they are able to work in renewables should they wish to (or choose a different path).

What we need is everyone empowered to do what they are able at this crucially important moment in time. This is our "What did you do in the war?" moment, recruiting us as active participants in positive change as we say to each other, "Let's do as much as we are able to help." What an incredible opportunity we have right here and now to be part of this moment in history, to say, *In my small way, I helped to save the planet.* Instead of looking to the future and despairing, maybe we can try to focus on the present and feel incredibly resolved.

It's worth remembering, too, not simply what we're fighting *against*, whether that's deforestation or new oil pipelines, but the good future we are fighting for. It helps to imagine that better world, with greener cities filled with free public transport and localized renewable energy networks, with vertical forests and moss walls removing carbon dioxide from the atmosphere, in a rewilded world filled with species recovering and ecosystems healing, where economic inequality, racism, and colonialism have been acknowledged and are addressed. Just because we don't know exactly how we'll get there, it doesn't mean that we can't take a step tomorrow in that direction. And then another. And another.

I hope you can forgive me for having the audacity to see a positive side to the climate crisis, but I love that it has focused us on our beautiful planet, so that we might no longer take it for granted. This is a gift. Another is the way that people are coming together on climate and environmental action. We do have a fight on our hands, but we're not alone. We can stand together to defend our home and pour our expertise, imagination, and energy into finding ways forward.

Greta Thunberg is only one of many of the younger generation asking us all to step up. Another is eleven-year-old activist Thierry Spall, who has been interested in wildlife since he was very young. When Thierry was eight, he began to notice that the David Attenborough programs he loved were "tinged with sadness" and that Attenborough had "begun to speak out about the catastrophic effects of climate change." Thierry was deeply affected by what he saw when "they started to show these scenes of people destroying the rain forest and logging and killing animals. I realized I had to do something about it because it wasn't just pictures on a screen, it was really happening." Thierry spoke to his teacher and made an announcement about the issues in front of his class. They collectively agreed that they should deliver an assembly to the rest of the school about what needed to happen to deal with climate change.

Thierry went to his first youth climate march with his dad and two friends in March 2019 and then began going to local campaign meetings with his mum Mira, who enjoyed the "relief of talking about it." The group shared gentle ways of explaining to people how they might do things differently. One example was making little cards to give to people to ask them to turn their car engines off when they were waiting outside shops or schools. Mira found that approaching them in this way usually meant that "people were nice about it." It made her feel hopeful that things could change for the better. In April 2019, Thierry joined a protest in Central London.

In Marble Arch, he got a chance to voice his concerns about climate change and his hopes for the future:

> *I spoke on the same stage as Greta Thunberg. There were about seven hundred people watching, and I was pretty nervous. I was the only child on the stage, and when I said I was only eleven, I got a big cheer. It made me happy, and it made me want to do more.*

Around the world, the children and young people taking part in these kinds of campaign may differ in race, ethnicity, gender, sexual orientation, socioeconomic status, physical abilities, and religious beliefs, but they're all making entirely reasonable demands of us. They're asking us to lay down arms, to treat them fairly, equally, without prejudice, to give them education and opportunities, to quit destroying the forests, to stop polluting the air and the oceans, to take care of animals, to just give them a glass of clean water. They are asking us to give them back their future and to give them hope. By doing so—as we act—we create hope for ourselves too. We mustn't give up on our own power to make positive change or let cynicism spread in us like a wildfire of despair. As Caitlin Moran says in her book *How to Build a Girl*, "Cynicism means you presume everything will end in disappointment." With that attitude, it follows that there's no point in even trying. Luckily, there are plenty of people not giving in to cynicism.

On October 31, 2018, a group known as Extinction Rebellion gathered in London, the first of many actions the international movement would take around the world to protest government inaction and raise awareness. This group holds to nonviolent principles and its main goals, in brief, are: for government to tell the truth by declaring an ecological and climate emergency; to act now to reduce greenhouse gas emissions and halt the loss of biodiversity; and for government to create and be led by a citizens' assembly on climate and ecological justice. Other groups have comparable aims such as the optimistic Sunrise Movement in the U.S. and the Climdev-Africa Youth Platform.

During the October 2019 Extinction Rebellion protest in London, I volunteered to help with "arrestee support" at a nearby police station—taking care of people as they got released from custody, giving them food and hot drinks and making sure they got home safely. As I arrived, my colleague told me about a woman in her eighties she'd just met who had traveled all the way from her home in Devon to join the protests in central London. I was impressed. I hoped I would be that committed as an octogenarian. When I talked to a few of my friends about the protest, some were cynical. They wondered how the protestors could afford to be there—didn't they have jobs? How did they have that much spare time? They asked me: Isn't it just attention-seeking? What good is it going to do? The fact is that many of the people I met over those few evenings had gone through considerable discomfort, becoming wet and cold during sleepless nights camping in flimsy tents on hard, damp floors. Most were not wealthy; some had taken unpaid leave to be able to join the protest, feeling strongly enough to make that sacrifice. There's no doubt that getting arrested involves much more risk for some people than others, but if those who can do it, do, and if their arrests result in political change, more widespread awareness or help to put these issues at the top of the agenda, then they are doing it for the good of all of us.

The people of all ages at these gatherings all over the world—the doctors, students, engineers, financiers, shop workers, the scientists, bartenders, artists, teachers—are angry, sad, and passionate because they care. The "grief and rage" as expressed by Extinction Rebellion is honest and important. As one of the founders of the movement, Gail Bradbrook, said in a speech she gave in London in July 2019 when talking about her sadness over the declining numbers of house sparrows in Britain—"love has a cost, and it's grief."

Yet the people taking part in these protests also expressed a beautiful, defiant hope. All of the protestors were there not because they were certain they'd get what they wanted, but because, in the words of playwright and president Václav Havel, they "work for something because it is good, not just because it stands a chance to succeed."

It seems people across the world are listening, with increasing numbers of us swelling the ranks of citizens making these vital calls for government action. In the week of September 20–27, 2019, international strikes and protests demanding action to address climate change took place in 150 countries. More than two thousand scientists in forty countries pledged to support the strikes, with an estimated 6 to 7.6 million people participating. The protests on September 20 were reported to be the largest climate strikes in world history.

Sometimes, of course, you can have doubts, and marches might feel hopeless. I have been on so many and have at times wondered at their purpose. Yet a vital and often overlooked part of the importance of assembling with strangers who broadly have the same aims as you—at a demonstration, a meeting, a rally, or a march, whatever the cause—is being reminded that you're not alone. Here are all those other people who care about the same things as you do. In his poem "The Masque of Anarchy," Percy Bysshe Shelley wrote about how witnessing this and being a part of it can give you hope.

> *Rise like lions after slumber*
> *In unvanquishable number—*
> *Shake your chains to earth like dew*
> *Which in sleep had fallen on you—*
> *Ye are many—they are few.*

I'm aware that the marching part is not for everyone, but the wider movement to save our wildlife, our green places and spaces, and our environment at large does have something for each one of us. After all, we are protecting our home.

When it comes to the climate and ecological emergencies, structural and systemic reform at scale by governments and companies across the world is essential. Nevertheless, there are many things we can do on an individual level beyond direct action.

MY OFFER

It's worth reminding yourself firstly that you don't have to singlehandedly fix the world. Whatever you can offer with your available time, money, and resources is welcome and wonderful. Identifying the skills and talents you already have will allow you to experience the pleasure of contributing with a clear purpose. You can have every hope of making a valuable contribution as you know what you can do. Here are some simple examples. They are small, yes, but if they're replicated many times over, they could result in real positive change. So invite others to do the same.

Share what you've learned: If you're good at talking, be sure to tell your family and friends about what you've learned and any changes you're making and why. We're much more likely to be influenced by those around us—and the ripple effect of this could go way beyond your close circle. Ask them to join you, donate to, or support a cause. Don't be afraid to challenge beliefs or behaviors that you disagree with, but do so gently, making sure you listen to those views.

Get campaigning: If you're great at writing, compile letters, emails, or even start a petition. Lobby your local politicians and council members and ask them to campaign for and act upon greener politics and policies. Let people know you've written and ask them to do the same. Go public with the letters and emails you've sent—share on social media and via your networks and connections exactly who you have contacted and why. This makes it much harder to ignore—using the power and reach of the internet for good.

Be practical: If you're great at DIY, try insulating your loft and walls, installing solar panels at home or maybe even at your school or community center. Use your carpentry skills to make a beehive, a bat box, or a raised bed for planting vegetables—and offer to teach others to do the same. Help people repair and transform things as an antidote to a throwaway culture and all the harm it causes.

Get creative: If you're artistic, use those skills to spread the message of positive change. Make posters to put up in your neighborhood with tips on small changes that can be made to counter climate change. Write a blog, make a film, create a podcast with tips and suggestions of how and what to do to help the cause and share widely. Use your creativity and your imagination to share ideas.

Get people together: If you're sociable and good at organizing, throw a party to raise funds and/or awareness for environmental and climate issues. Have a "swap shop" party where people exchange clothes and goods. Have a clear out and offer what you can for free. Put on a climate crisis film night at your community center and let people know what green initiatives and projects are happening in your neighborhood.

A few years ago, I thought about what I could offer to help the environment. I had a little spare time, some plant knowledge, and a love of being outdoors. I wanted to find something I'd enjoy and that would be easy to keep doing. Something active and hopeful outside of demonstrations.

Like many people, I've always loved trees. So that's where I began. I started planting trees in my area, helping our local park group, and adored it—it was a free workout and immensely satisfying.

Humbling, too, to realize that with a bit of luck the trees I helped to plant would outlast me by hundreds of years.

As I planted, I began to find out a lot more about trees, such as how they clean the air around us by absorbing pollutants such as nitrogen oxides, ammonia, sulfur dioxide, and ozone. They also filter potentially harmful air particulates by trapping them on their leaves and bark. In one year, one acre of mature trees can absorb the same amount of CO_2 as is produced by driving your car twenty-six thousand miles and can provide enough oxygen for eighteen people. Trees improve the local area—not just for us but for our local wildlife too, providing a home and food for birds, bees, and squirrels as well as other flora and fauna, and having a cooling effect.

It was when working alongside others in my park group that I first came across Trees for Cities, a charity that specializes in planting urban trees. Seb, their urban forest manager, told me that they had already planted their millionth tree in 2018 at St. Mary's Hospital at Westminster Bridge.

Today I'm a volunteer tree-planting supervisor for Trees for Cities, helping people who come along to their events, and in December 2018, I took part in London's largest-ever planting project, during which we bedded in twenty-five thousand trees across four sites in a weekend. It's wonderful in so many ways. There's a real sense of collective spirit and such diversity among the people who take part who, as I've found, plant trees for all sorts of reasons. Many, like me, want to do something tangible to help the environment, some enjoy being outdoors, others simply love trees or come out of curiosity or a desire to have a new experience.

On a recent planting day, we chatted as we dug, about the environment and hope. We talked about how some people question the point of planting one tree in times of such epic deforestation. Dan (aged seventy-three, the fastest digger in the team) said, "Well, doing something is always better than doing nothing," and he was rewarded with a cheer. We discussed what would happen if one person who planted a tree could then persuade someone else to do the same, and so on—imagine. One million people each planting a tree in their garden—now, that would be transformative. It would turn cities into forests. So, those of us lucky enough to have gardens all pledged that day to each plant a tree and to pass on the baton. A quiet revolution had begun.

Tree planting is everywhere. The Schools Trees Project in Jinja, Uganda, is a small but mighty organization tackling deforestation and the wider environmental crisis head-on. The project was started by Ronald Kiwalabye, who wanted to "take the fight against climate change right into schools in Uganda," including their Seeds for Future campaign. Sixteen schools in the Jinja and Iganga districts of Uganda have taken part, raising 2,106 fruit trees from seed. They also have a renewable energy program aimed at reducing an overdependence on firewood, the country's leading source of deforestation. Children are taught how to make charcoal alternatives from soil and charcoal dust. There are also Green Corps environmental clubs run by the children in villages. They raise their own seedlings and plant trees in their communities, performing educational dramas about climate change as a way of sharing information.

---

try this:
FAMILY TREE

There are projects like the ones in Deptford, London, and in Jinja, Uganda, all over the world. The chances are there is a tree-planting project near to you, so if you fancy joining a group, start investigating. Local libraries, parks, and community groups may be able to help you find one. In the U.S., One Tree Planted has planted trees in more than a dozen U.S. states and across three Canadian provinces. American Forests' amazing work includes working with local partners in cities to convert vacant space into accessible green space by planting trees. For more organizations and information, take a look at the chapter notes at the end of the book.

There are lots of amazing smaller tree-planting projects going on globally, but there is room for a lot more. The Trillion Tree Campaign was launched in 2006, inspired by Nobel Peace Laureate and founder of the Green Belt Movement Wangari Maathai, who said, "It is the little things that citizens do. That's what will make the difference. My little thing is planting trees." The billionth tree, an African olive, was planted in Ethiopia in 2007. This campaign in turn led to the United Nation's Trillion Tree Campaign, and in November 2019, their website registered over 13.6 billion trees planted in over 193 countries.

So what effect can all this tree planting have? Scientists agree that planting billions of trees across the world is one of the most effective and cheapest ways of taking CO_2 out of the atmosphere and thereby tackling the climate crisis. New research has found that a worldwide planting initiative could remove an estimated two thirds of all the human-generated emissions that remain in the atmosphere today. Granted, even with all these new trees, it's still vital to reverse rising greenhouse gases right now, flattening them to net zero as quickly as possible, because the forest restoration envisaged would take between fifty and one hundred years to have its full effect. Yet, in so many different countries, trees are being embraced as a sign of our collective responsibility and collective joy in the natural world. As people plant together, as I saw firsthand, connections are made, communities strengthened, new ways of living envisaged, shoots of hope carefully tended.

try this:
LITTLE ACORNS

If you're keen to get going in your own garden, here are some trees you could try. (Don't plant an American redwood in your pocket-hanky-sized backyard, as they can grow to up to 350 feet high and can achieve a diameter of 23 feet!).

According to the Tree Council, it's a good idea when choosing a species to "copy nature by planting trees already successful on or near the site." So have a look at what's around you already. According to Seb and Trees for Cities, buying a tree grown locally is best too, as trees imported from other countries may bring with them pests and diseases that could spread to other trees.

Some good tree choices for small gardens include:

- flowering cherry tree ,
- dogwood tree
- Japanese maple
- paperbark maple tree
- serviceberry tree
- crabapple tree

If you'd love to get involved but for whatever reason you're not able to plant trees, here are a few other ways you can help protect forests around the world.

Help the rain forests by avoiding unsustainable palm oil—so often the cause of large-scale deforestation.

Look out for RSPO-certified sustainable palm oil rather than rejecting all palm oil, as some alternatives take much more land to produce.

Choose recycled toilet paper, printer paper, or tree-free paper (made from waste straw and hemp, so not one tree is cut down).

Cut down on beef—most fast food burgers are made of beef from cattle grazed on land cleared of trees in the rain forest. If there is less demand, there's less reason to clear the forest for the cattle.

Helping trees in some way, however and whenever you're able to, is only ever going to be a good thing. Nevertheless, as Seb from Trees for Cities made clear, it is important to know that this isn't all about individual responsibility:

We don't want people to feel it is all down to them—we all have to make little differences where we can, but it's also got to be about spreading awareness. We have to be aware that all the things we are doing, like recycling or becoming a vegan, these things are amazing but they are a drop in the ocean compared to what governments and corporations should be doing. As soon as you change policy, that's when stuff changes. We can email our councilors and lobby politicians, go on marches and

demonstrations, and let each other know that we do have the
power to change things if we stick together.

Shockingly, just one hundred companies are responsible for 71 percent of global emissions. We cannot allow them to carry on with business as usual or to "greenwash" their actions. Nor should we expect less from our governments than we do from ourselves or the people around us. Some global leaders might well be relieved if we turned on one another for not being or doing enough, drawing attention away from their part in all of this. What is amazingly hopeful is that we now have the green technology and the ecological solutions to meet this challenge if we act with the urgency the situation requires. What is now vital is the corporate and political will; we have to push for this, challenging our leaders and demanding change. As Bishop Desmond Tutu said, "There comes a point where we need to stop just pulling people out of the river. We need to go upstream and find out why they're falling in." Yet if we "go upstream" and discover that those in power are not helping, where do we find hope then?

In Australia in 2019 a series of devastating bushfires began. As of January 14, 2020, an estimated eighteen million hectares had been burned and at least thirty-three people and approximately one billion animals killed, with some species in danger of extinction. As of January 2, 2020, NASA estimated that 306 million tons of CO_2 had been emitted from the ravaged forests. It was a desperately sad and worrying situation.

The "upstream" reason that the Australian bushfires were so ruinous and widespread is widely acknowledged by scientists to be due to climate change. Seemingly in denial of these facts, the Australian prime minister, Scott Morrison, described targets and goals to slow global heating as "job-destroying, economy-destroying, economy-wrecking." People rallied in Sydney in December 2019 against government inaction on this issue, carrying homemade banners saying "No profit on a dead planet" while their country burned and the prime minister enjoyed a family holiday in Hawaii.

In early January 2020, in the town of Wentworth Falls in the Blue Mountains region of New South Wales, Mayor Mark Greenhill addressed a packed community meeting. The New South Wales Rural Fire Service, alongside other agencies, was working tirelessly around the clock to contain and manage the fires. He paid tribute to the firefighters "both paid and unpaid" who had been "defending us, putting their safety on the line for us...for months, day after day, night after night. It is a level of community service that dwarves anything that anyone like myself will ever do." In the meeting, Mayor Greenhill also paid tribute to the collective action of the people of the Blue Mountains, saying, "It is hard to move in a fire shed at the moment because of the huge generosity and donations flowing in to sustain our firefighters from all of you." The people of the Blue Mountains pulled together under the very toughest of circumstances to see each other through.

Adam Bullock, Rebecca Cooper, and their children are residents of Springwood, a Blue Mountains town. They'd come to England for Christmas to visit family and I spoke to them as they were waiting at the airport in Heathrow, unsure of what they might find on their return.

Adam told me: "We can't seem to depend on our government anymore, so we help ourselves, which is beautiful but...we would be letting them off the hook if we didn't challenge them as well." Adam said that despite a lack of leadership from their prime minister on climate issues, his community did feel supported by different kinds of leaders. He told me:

> *Our local representatives Trish Doyle and Susan Templeman are out on the front line every day talking to people, and the mayor, Mark Greenhill, is at all the planning meetings with the firefighters. They are amazing. It was so encouraging to know that they cared... We just want a modern, well-thought-out policy around renewable energies, so we can get rid of this reliance on coal and fossil. I'm looking for a change of government, as I don't have any hope that this one is going to change.*

try this:
FIND A HOPE PARTY

In the face of incompetent, weak, or destructive leaders, the truth is we can no longer wait for the ballot box and the hope of a different government in the future to effect change. We need to get involved now. If current leadership is making you despair, find out which alternative offers you hope, with policies and people whose ideas chime with your own (even if imperfectly). Go to meetings, support those who are reaching and working for a better future, persuade others to change their voting intentions by discussing your point of view.

Adam compared Australia's approach to that of New Zealand, where Jacinda Ardern's landmark climate legislation passed in parliament with historic cross-party support, 119 votes to one. The bill commits New Zealand to reducing its carbon emissions to zero by 2050 and meet its commitments under the Paris climate accords, with the aim of keeping global heating below 1.5 degrees. She said, "I absolutely believe and continue to stand by the statement that climate change is the biggest challenge of our time."

The legislation was celebrated by environmental groups all over the world, acknowledging that New Zealand is leading the world in its approach to the climate crisis. If you listened carefully, you could hear the cheers of concerned citizens, environmentalists, and green activists everywhere. Our current climate crisis is a complicated issue. We can, however, use the same tools of scientific innovation and international action as we have done before—and there is hope in that. And there is huge hope in the knowledge that it's not too late to take action that will help the environment and millions, even billions, of people, now and in the future.

We have to do what we can as individuals and put pressure on those in power to act. Our scientists should be listened to and their advice heeded. We can invest in further green energy innovation and ecological restoration while dramatically reducing our fossil fuel emissions and increasing biodiversity. We can choose a sustainable future built upon social and climate justice. Every degree of global heating that we prevent matters. We have all that we need to get to work and we can all play our part. Climate change reminds us that we can't change the world on our own, but there is certainly the hope that we can do it together.

CHAPTER NINE
back to the future

FINDING HOPE FOR TOMORROW IN SCIENCE,
ART, AND INNOVATION

....

"THE FUTURE BELONGS
TO THOSE WHO BELIEVE IN
THE BEAUTY OF THEIR DREAMS."

—ELEANOR ROOSEVELT

O<small>N</small> J<small>ULY</small> 16, 1969, <small>AT</small> 8:32 a.m. (EST), the Apollo 11 space vehicle was launched from Florida, USA. Its mission: to put the first human on the surface of the moon.

We have always looked up at the night sky in awe and wonder. The moon is the largest and brightest object in our night sky and our fascination with its mystery is clear in our many myths and stories— it's associated with divinity, madness, and beastly transformations. The moon looms large and ghostly silver in our imaginations. But it had remained remote, unknowable, and unreachable—until now.

For several days before, members of the public had begun to camp out on the beaches of Florida's Space Coast, eager to get a good spot to witness the realization of humankind's long-cherished dream. By launch day, over one million people had gathered, all filled with excitement as they watched history being made. Some 600 million people, around a sixth of the world's population at that time, watched on TV as Neil Armstrong took his first steps on the moon's surface.

The moon landing was a triumph of hope and optimism. It may have been partly driven by the fierce competition between the USA and the USSR during the Cold War, but it was only made possible by the courage and vision of a community of scientists, engineers, and technicians from all over the world, creating a truly global achievement.

People were in awe of what we humans were capable of achieving. Speaking on the BBC *Panorama* episode "Apollo 11: The Impact on Earth," the economist Barbara Ward said she drew hope from it because it countered the terrifying menace of the nuclear arms race. She thought that the images of our beautiful blue planet, tiny and precious in the vast darkness of space, might help us realize how fortunate we are to live here, creating the opportunity to bring a divided world together:

> *It's the first time the human race has been able to see in its imagination where it actually lives, how small, how shining, how vulnerable, how real it is, and if it's true that we change nothing until we change our imaginations...I think this is the first step toward us changing how we think about ourselves.*

This was a time when people were optimistic about the future, when, as expressed by the hero of the sci-fi film *Tomorrowland*, we all dreamed of "blue skies and jet packs and hope." We were confident in the ability of our technology and innovation to serve the common good, to overcome seemingly insurmountable problems. We began to imagine what might come next—was this the dawning of a new age of wonders? If science could put a man on the moon, surely there was a way to use it to fix the problems we had on earth, such as poverty, famine, war, and racism? Thomas Paine, head of NASA administration, made this point in a TV interview at the time:

> Why aren't our political institutions bringing to people around the world this great common aspiration—that we all have freedom from hunger and ignorance and disease; why can't we be better at many of these other areas as well as reach out and touch the moon?

The potential we envisaged in our future progress was clear in the stories we told back then: science fiction presented us with hopeful, aspirational views of the future that showed humanity at its best. Okay, they may have been cheating a little bit by neatly skipping over the scientific and technical innovations and political choices that would make any of this possible. Nevertheless, as we've touched on before, we have to imagine a thing first before we can begin taking steps to make it a reality. Submarines, mobile phones, 3D printers—all of these began their lives as imaginary inventions in science fiction.

A great example of a hopeful future was *Star Trek*. In it, creator Gene Roddenberry expressed his vision for a future in which hunger, prejudice, and war were eradicated, freeing us up to focus on exploration and the pursuit of knowledge. Like many other sci-fi visions of utopias, it presented an end to scarcity, which allowed us to be our best selves. The TV series first aired in 1966, at the height of the Cold War and in the midst of the war with Vietnam, with the continuing struggles of the civil rights movement in the background. The bridge crew of the Enterprise included Russian ensign Pavel Andreievich Chekov (pretty radical at the height of the Cold War), Japanese American Lieutenant Hikaru Sulu (only twenty-five years after the attack on Pearl Harbor), and Lieutenant Nyota Uhura, played by the young black actress Nichelle Nichols. When considering whether to quit the show, Dr. Martin Luther King Jr. told Nichols that she couldn't leave because she was a powerful role model for millions of Black women and girls at a time when it was rare to see a Black actor in a prominent and powerful position. At such a time, to propose that we were capable of living in peace, and for different races and nationalities to coexist harmoniously, was certainly a bold and optimistic assertion.

Stories such as these can inspire us, as Jayne Nelson, features editor of *SFX* magazine and *Star Trek* fan told me, "When I was a child, I held high hopes that one day we'd be as noble as the heroes I saw on *Star Trek*... It was such an aspirational worldview! Sci-fi can sometimes be so bleak—think *Blade Runner* or *Alien*—that it's great to see positive stories."

try this:
FUTURE PERFECT

What did you imagine the future would be like as a child? If you liked sci-fi or fantasy, what were your favorite stories or films? Were you excited by the thought of moon travel or robots? Were there any particular inventions you wanted to become reality—and have they? Consider how the scientific and technological innovations that have come into being in your lifetime have benefited you personally and/or society as a whole in positive ways. Reminding ourselves of the incredible inventions humans have come up with can help us to be hopeful for our future: look at all the good we've already done, look at all the wonders we've already created.

Next focus on what you hope for the future now. What would a future utopia be like for you? Let yourself dream big. Later, we'll revisit these hopes and see how they might be realized.

You may be thinking, yes, that was nice, and it's all very well for science fiction creators to imagine a future where everything is rosy, but there's a long way to go from imagining something to making it a reality. Who and what can deliver these utopias, and how might we help? Before we investigate that, let's look for a moment at the tales that we're telling ourselves about the future today. There's the bleak dystopia portrayed in stories such as Cormac McCarthy's novel *The Road*, in which a boy and his father endure a desperate struggle for survival in a world in ruins; the TV series *The Walking Dead*, which suggests a future world riddled with zombies—but the real monsters are the human survivors. Even superheroes aren't what they used to be when they were created in the 1950s and '60s. The recent TV series *The Boys* depicts some of them as corrupt, amoral narcissists. When I spoke with "Trekkie" Rich Matthews, he expressed concern that even some of the more recent Star Trek work has a "creeping darkness" to it.

I wonder if this is because we're losing faith in ourselves and in our capability to be good. Perhaps our fears and anxieties of conflict, war, and climate change have infected even our most optimistic science fiction. Maybe the stories we hear, share, and tell about each other via the news, social media, and popular culture encourage this pessimism. Our current reality can make it hard to be hopeful about the future with so much on our minds: extreme weather events, health, the environment, the economy, our children's safety, job security, racism, sexism—the list goes on. According to a Pew Research study in America, it does seem that some of us have become pessimistic about the future. Looking ahead to 2050 the study revealed only 56 percent feel optimistic about the situation thirty years from now, and on specific topics such as the environment and healthcare, the majority were pessimistic. A huge 73 percent expect the gap between rich and poor to have increased.

In the face of all our challenges, how is it possible for us to find a way to proceed with optimism? We need our hope to be under-pinned by *real* innovations, inventions, experiences, and positive changes that we can benefit from, contribute to, and engage with right now. We need to be informed about current scientific and technological innovations that have the potential to create a better future world. We can depend on science and scientists, who don't require us to have blind faith but present us with facts and practical solutions with which we can engage.

try this:
SCIENCE FACT

Let's revisit your hopes for the future and get science's help! Microbiologist Louis Pasteur said, "Science...is the torch which illuminates the world"—it can provide us with light in the darkness of despair. The technology you're hoping for in the future may well already be in development.

There are plenty of ways you can find out more, even if you've never studied science, or have found it baffling or intimidating in the past. Many universities have free public talks and lectures as part of their community and outreach programs, so go along or watch them online— they're designed to be friendly and accessible. Kids' science books and programs are a great start too. Check out the TV programs about science innovation, subscribe to free newsletters (*Scientific American* is a great example), and don't be afraid to ask questions whenever you can (Einstein told us, "The important thing is to not stop questioning"). You might even want to consider a free online course—plenty of institutions offer them on many topics such as climate science, AI tech, and space science. Many of the challenges we face are being addressed and researched by scientists all over the world right now, with some astonishing results.

Of course, science and technology doesn't always get things right. Consider the story of plastic. Poor old plastic, our man-made polymer nemesis, the substance that hardly anyone loves anymore, although it had a benign and hopeful genesis. Inspired by a New York business offering $10,000 (a fortune back in 1869) to anyone who could invent a substitute for ivory, amateur inventor John Wesley Hyatt created the first synthetic polymer, a plastic which was created by treating cellulose with camphor. Shortly afterward, advertisements praised his invention as the savior of the wild elephant and the tortoise, as this new material could be made to imitate not only ivory but tortoiseshell and horn too. It looked like the new-fangled plastics could protect the natural world from the destructive forces of humans. Plastic really was fantastic back then—it made early film possible (with the development of celluloid), improved hygiene, helped with the preservation of food and medicine, and it was long-lasting and easy to clean.

Plastic is one of humankind's incredibly creative and ingenious responses to a particular problem. Unfortunately, it's also an example of an invention that itself became problematic (much like other troublemakers such as the fossil-fuel-hungry combustion engine, nuclear energy, and pesticides, to name a few). As early as the 1960s the first plastic debris in the oceans was observed. I'm as sure as I can be, given that I've never met him, that John Wesley Hyatt did not intend to pollute the sea and endanger marine wildlife with his creation. Nevertheless, we're all well aware of the problem with plastic now, and it has become a metaphor for everything cheap, disposable, contemptible, and bad. What we can learn from this is that we should look into the future, to consider what the consequences of our actions might be, in the short, medium, and long term, and consider wherever possible the impact of our scientific and technological innovations on the world at large.

However, we humans are endlessly creative and brilliant problem solvers. We never really give up on our troublesome inventions, and there is always someone somewhere trying to fix problems we've created. In the case of plastic and pollution, science and innovation may still be the key to solving the issue.

Boyan Slat, a young Dutch inventor, launches his nearly two-thousand-foot-long floating rubbish-collector, and collects all the plastic from the sea. When he gets it back home to Holland, he transports it to the city of Zwolle, where it's made into bike paths that are installed in cities all over the world. An Indonesian start-up called Evoware has created seaweed packaging that can replace plastic. A group of microbiologists at Quaid-i-Azam University in Pakistan has discovered a fungus that could consume existing plastic in landfills. In a small town on a tiny island off Panama, a group of residents led by Robert Bezeau collect plastic bottles off their beaches, which are transformed into buildings forming the stylish and eco-friendly Plastic Bottle Village. Setting sail from Kenya to Zanzibar in September 2018 was the world's first boat made entirely from recycled plastic.

"All science is rooted in hope," said Dr. Kimberley Trim, a cellular biologist and research strategy coordinator at Imperial College London. "Even though there is this funny pop culture trope of the evil genius of a mad scientist playing god with no respect for common human values, the intention of the vast majority of scientists is to make life better for people and planet."

So if we can agree that although we've made mistakes and messed things up, for the most part, it's been with the best of intentions, and we're making progress. We can find and share a vision of the future which doesn't entail us "sitting under dripping, apocalyptic railway bridges eating dry quinoa" (a tongue-in-cheek fear expressed by my sci-fi writer friend Paul Arvidson), but one that's fun, joyful, and inclusive, that's underpinned by real-life innovations and initiatives. If we know a little more about some of the projects already underway, this will provide us with hope for the future, as we see that our prospects are not as bleak as they might seem.

try this:
DON'T BE AFRAID OF THE DARK

What are your fears about the future? Perhaps it's how we can feed the world's growing population, for example, or the rise of antibiotic-resistant bacteria. Your fears can be scary things to think about, I know, so once you have identified yours, look for what's being done to offer possible solutions. Right now, all over the world, there are incredible people and organizations seeking answers and taking action. Finding the people who share your concern and discovering what they're doing about it will help you feel hopeful that there's a way forward. These are the people, like us, who have not given up on the future. Seek them out. Listen to their stories. Tell them yours. Join them.

One thing that comes up time and time again when I'm talking with people about their worries for the present and the future is that our relationship with tech is disconnecting us from each other and the outside world. It's worth remembering here how tech helped us during the coronavirus pandemic, enabling many of us to do a number of key things: to stay connected during lockdown, to continue working, to teach our kids and keep us entertained. Technology was one of the tools that facilitated a blossoming of collective creative expression during this dark time too, including online play readings, group movement classes, and concerts where whole orchestras played together online while isolated in their own homes. Yet even before the virus pandemic, there were plenty of stories demonstrating how tech can help us connect.

Ashley James Brown is a creative coder, technologist, and artist with whom I worked at the digital arts festival Frequency, in Lincoln UK in 2019. All of Ashley's work is concerned with nostalgia, empathy, and human connection. He and Samantha Lindley of Threshold Studios dreamt up the idea of repurposing a 1990s arcade game to create a new version that would touch upon mental health, particularly in men of the generation that played on this kind of game as kids. Their overriding purpose was to "encourage kindness." They named their game Eleos, after the Greek goddess of compassion. Players are encouraged to help the characters they encounter in the game, discovering what they might need, finding it, and delivering it to them. To go up a level in the game, you're given a card on which is an invitation to carry out an act of kindness in the real world. My small contribution to this amazing project was to devise the hundred or so acts of kindness to be printed on the cards.

The prototype of Eleos was up and running during the festival, and hundreds of people tried it out and loved it. The TV presenter Jason Bradbury came and played it too and filmed himself having a chat with and buying a cup of tea for a homeless man as he accepted his kindness mission.

Ashley imagines that in the near future, tech could allow us to experience a wide range of physical realities different to our own, to encourage compassion and awareness. One of his other experimental projects is an Empathy Jacket, which simulates the experience of Parkinson's disease so the wearer can gain a greater understanding of the condition and what other people are going through. There are already plenty of other examples, including a virtual reality technology called Care(less) created by artist Lindsay Seers, which "gives you the opportunity to feel what it might be like to be in the body of an older person facing a gradual reduction in capacity." The experience enables us to contemplate attitudes to aging and what it means to be cared for. A Mile in My Shoes, part of the Empathy Museum project by artist Clare Patey, is an immersive experience in which visitors are invited to literally walk a mile in someone else's shoes while listening, on a headset, to that person's story in their own voice and words, from a Syrian refugee to a sex worker, a war veteran to a neurosurgeon.

Scientists, product designers, engineers, and doctors are also exploring ways to create quality care for people with dementia. In the UK, the Alzheimer's Society pledged £50 million to the UK Dementia

Research Institute's Care Research and Technology Center, which is developing technologies to create dementia-friendly homes. This includes robotic devices that will interact with people and alert them to dangers such as spilled liquid or a stove burner that has been left on. In the future, sensors will allow researchers to monitor people's blood pressure, heart rate, and temperatures in their own homes, so that their medical teams can be aware of any potential problems at an early stage. AI will also pick up on any changes that might indicate a patient is at immediate risk, for example by detecting "an elevated temperature that could suggest an infection." These technologies aren't intended to replace human contact but rather to offer additional support, to allow people to live as independently as possible.

There is plenty of evidence that science and tech can serve to keep us connected and encourage empathy, but I wanted to find out where and how they might deliver the utopia promised by some sci-fi visions. One of my own major concerns is around food. I'd read and seen so much alarming news about how we're not going to be able to feed anywhere near everyone into the future with our present systems, an ever-rising population, crops hindered by climate change, and huge quantities of food waste. There's a broad consensus that there just isn't enough appropriate land mass to support our current practices of meat and dairy farming, which take up enormous amounts of space and water, often at the expense of wildlife and the local ecosystems that sustain it and us.

To avoid falling into despair, I took my own advice and investigated what's being done to address this. I looked to the future of farming to see what we might change. There are different approaches and contradictory ideas out there—all part of the journey as we try to work out the sticky business of feeding the world while protecting the planet—but I discovered many innovations that provide flickers of hope. One possible solution is a farm-free golden-colored wonder product developed by Finnish scientists, with tech inspired by the space industry. The company, Solar Foods, pulls carbon dioxide out of the atmosphere, to which they add water, bacteria, and renewable electricity to trigger fermentation that yields a high-protein flour-like substance called Solein. It has many potential uses, including as an ingredient in bread and pasta, and because it's so high in protein, it could become a viable meat alternative.

The company says it's "bringing a completely new harvest to humankind," and is aiming to produce two million meals a year by 2021 and then scale up to provide a protein source to nine billion people by 2050. Solein can be created anywhere in the world; it doesn't require fertile land or very much water, and all the processing comes from renewable resources, so this space-age food could be vital for countries facing food shortages, droughts or natural disasters. Whether they manage to do this, and whether we will embrace this new food source, only time will tell, but that such passion and energy is being dedicated to solving our food problems is in itself cause to be hopeful: there are people out there trying to fix this.

As for our vegetables, it could be that many will be grown in hydroponic or vertical farms, in disused urban spaces, where their roots are misted rather than submerged in soil. Vertical farms mean less widespread soil degradation, and they could provide local food within cities all year round and in places where the space to grow food in soil is limited. In places including Bellevue and Kirkland, Washington, there are already some supermarkets with in-store hydroponic farms.

These ideas are interesting, no doubt, but I wonder whether reconnecting with our food production and embracing more natural processes might be a better approach, allowing us to reap the proven mental and physical health benefits at the same time. As Henry Beston wrote in his novel *The Outermost House*, we are "remote from universal nature and living by complicated artifice" and perhaps this is part of what got us into this mess in the first place.

I came across two wonderful developments that seem to be moving us in a more connected direction. The first is the growing trend of eco-agriculture—a more traditional type of farming which pays attention to the relationships between soil, animals, plants and microbes, and it's gaining in popularity worldwide. A wonderful example is happening in Mali, West Africa, where degraded agricultural lands have been restored. Here crops are grown and animals grazed among naturally regenerated trees, which help to restore the soil with their leaf drop. The trees help the soil absorb moisture, protect it from wind and water erosion, and provide shade to the land and grazing animals. These practices also help the land adapt to climate change, acting as "carbon sinks." In the UK, Swillington Organic Farm is home to free-range farm animals as well as providing a haven for wildlife and habitats including woodland, marsh, pasture, and ponds. Carefully managed grazing means that the farm animals can benefit the local nature reserve, and all of the produce is organic. Their waste helps fertilize the ground and provides a good habitat for dung beetles and other insects. There are studies in progress to demonstrate that these systems are sustainable and viable on a larger scale, including the five-year research project Agriculture at a Crossroads, which involves four hundred scientists from sixty countries.

The second idea is perhaps the most promising innovation in my eyes, because many of us could get directly involved in it right now. Frustrated by having to travel forty miles to buy an apple in his home in South Los Angeles, gardener Ron Finley took a vacant lot and planted fruit trees and vegetables on it. Ron discovered that the city owned vacant lots equivalent to twenty Central Parks, enough land to grow "725 million tomato plants." If we could grow our own food on those forlorn patches of land sprinkled all over our cities, imagine how many people that could feed and how much healthier the communities might be as a result. Ron said, "I have witnessed my garden transform my neighborhood" and he believes that we should all have the chance to experience "the joy, the pride, and the honor in growing your own food."

While I found some very different ideas and solutions to the "feed the world" dilemma—each with their detractors and critics—what they all have in common is a sincere desire to solve a problem, empower communities, and protect the planet, albeit in very different ways. Who knows what we could be eating in 2050—space pancakes? Organic ancient grains grown on a nearby eco-farm? Or veggies we've helped to grow in our community allotments? The sheer variety of ideas, solutions, and innovations on offer gives me hope that we can solve this.

So as you can see, there are many ingenious projects under development that could help us get to our brighter future—and those were just a few examples of countless projects underway in one industry. So let's take a moment to paint a hopeful picture of where all this might lead.

Let's say we've freed up huge amounts of land from grazing animals as we choose to eat less meat. Our herbs and vegetables grow in the air or in our own community spaces and gardens, as we learn to be farmers ourselves. Alternative protein sources are created cheaply and easily in labs and factories. Food is delicious and affordable, its production is carbon neutral, and there is plenty for everyone. Children pick apples in the orchards in their own schools. Farmland is rewilded, filled with an abundance of wildlife that happily coexists with crops. We have beautiful places to visit and work in, where we can breathe fresh, clean, unpolluted air, improving our physical and mental well-being and providing us with spaces for play, fun, celebration, contemplation, and memorial.

Meanwhile, in the cities all public transport is free and is run on renewable energy. The sound of engines has been replaced by birdsong, the clink of spoons against coffee cups and chattering children walking safely in crocodile lines to school. People walk and cycle, improving their physical and mental fitness. Access for wheelchair users, and for those with sensory and learning impairments too, are greatly improved. City dwellers breathe clean air thanks to trees everywhere, planted and cared for by the community.

Power is supplied by community-owned solar panels and solar paint on our homes. Everyone who has a garden or a window box grows their own food. Local shops sell boxes of wonky vegetables cheaply, reducing waste.

We have enough food, water, education, and space because we have achieved the cultural and spiritual transformation we needed by deciding to love each other, to educate ourselves and rid ourselves of negative bias and prejudices, to be kind, to be fair, to ensure equality for all. And this transformation includes all of us: CEOs, politicians, heads of industry, artists, scientists, teachers, farmers, refuse collectors, nurses, care workers, students, parents, kids. All it has taken is for each of us to persuade ourselves and each other that this kind of world is a better world to live in and then to act—in hope, with hope, creating hope—to make it happen.

This might be a world of my own creation, but there is no need for it to remain fictional. It is within our grasp. So much of it is based on things that are already happening. Public transport is already free in several cities in Europe, including Dunkerque, Tallinn, and Luxembourg. Downtown Pontevedra in Spain is already car-free. In the village of Aharkandhi in northeastern Bangladesh, residents have installed solar panels on their roofs, providing a cheaper source of electricity for all. In Taff Bargoed in Wales, a site that was home to three coal mines has been transformed into a community park and wildlife reserve, and the power of the river has been harnessed to produce hydropower, enough for the needs of 150 average-sized households. In Nairobi, Kenya, the fantastic organization Taka Taka collects waste from households, businesses, and factories. It turns organic waste into high-quality compost and recycles 95 percent of the other materials—one of the highest rates in the world.

With innovations such as these, combined with compassion, community, and hope, I believe we can make that utopia a reality.

You may have your own, quite different, hopeful vision of how the future could look. You might not agree with mine, and that's fine. We were never meant to work it all out on our own anyway. As I'm sure you've come to see, hope is an active, shared, collective endeavor. I have learned so much on this journey about what it takes, and what it will take, to make things better for ourselves, others, and the planet. It needs all of us, with our "I have an idea" and our "this just might work" and our "what about if we...?"

We need to accept and put aside our differences, to discover the things we have in common, and work together for a better future. We need to focus on what we want that future to look like and concentrate our efforts on making it happen. What a relief it will be for all of us to evolve from this highly individualistic place to a future where we understand that our collective action has the power to change everything for the better. We already have everything we need to achieve what we hope for; we only need to come together and summon the courage to act on our wildest dreams. We can do it.

EPILOGUE

a manifesto for hope

*T*HANK YOU FOR COMING WITH me on this journey. It's been a real privilege to speak with and listen to so many different people as I explored ways to find hope—and hold on to it. One of the most encouraging things for me as I discussed hope with friends and strangers was that a few core ideas kept cropping up, which came to form a kind of manifesto of hope for our times. So, to end, I wanted to share these with you here.

Courage: We can and should choose to be hopeful. But to do so, especially at times of hardship or adversity, requires courage. Be kind to yourself, start small, allow your courage and your hope to grow.

Purpose: Having a purpose or an aim gives us energy and focus, something specific and achievable to hope for and act upon. Purpose also gives meaning to our actions, which helps give us the energy to persevere.

Values: Knowing what we believe in and understanding why we're pursuing our purpose or aim gives us direction and focus, whatever comes our way. Knowing that we'll always be able to hold on to our values, that we'll be committed to them and give the best we can, fuels our hope.

Community: It's much easier to persevere if you have a group of like-minded people working toward a common goal. If you get tired or weary, you can let the group take over for a while, so it's not all on you. It's also more fun.

Action: Hope is believing in the possibility of change, and change requires action. Acting on our hopes creates more hope. Even small steps empower us and give us confidence.

Lastly, I think it's essential that we seek out, collect, and share all kinds of hopeful stories, to inspire ourselves and others, to help us find the patch of blue sky on a gloomy day. Living in hope, as I have discovered, is a happier way to live.

acknowledgments

Every time I write a thank-you list, I get nervous. I have never managed it without leaving someone out—so if this is you and you are reading it thinking "How very dare she?" please accept my sincere apologies. I am lucky and grateful to know such generous, well-read, and forgiving people.

First things first, thank you to my lovely agent Zoe King at AM Heath—looking forward to tea and cake at some point. Thanks for seeking me out, believing in me, and letting me jabber on about hope and kindness. Also to Julia Churchill for taking over when Zoe went on maternity leave. Thanks to the lovely team at my U.S. publisher, Sourcebooks, especially the warm and witty editor Erin McClary, associate managing editor Heather Hall, and art director Brittany Vibbert, who created the beautiful and inspiring cover. Thanks to my UK publisher, Elliott and Thompson, and the mind-boggling editing skills of Sarah Rigby and Pippa Crane. Thanks for all the advice, guidance, and pertinent questions and for infinite patience, kindness, and good humor. I especially want to thank Sarah for the sunny pre-COVID walk, chat, and really strong coffee in Walthamstow Wetlands, which reminded me how much I passionately wanted to defend hope. Thanks also to the fabulous Emma Finnigan for her PR wizardry, Ella Chapman for her brilliant marketing, Meg Humphries for copyediting, and to Marianne Thorndahl for her immense organizational talents.

For support, inspiration, and company on this journey, my huge love and eternal gratitude as ever go to my beloved Gareth Brierley and Lola who made sure that I left my desk to walk in Oxleas Woods with them every day.

Also huge thanks to Emma Waterford, Mark Stevenson, Kas Darley, and Sophie Austin (Teatro Vivo); Ed Cobbold and Eleanor Jones (Royal Albert Hall); Ian Toothill, Emma O'Rourke, Richard Barker, James Hodgson, Vanessa Roots, Cardboard Citizens, and Augustus Boal; Vanessa Woolf (London Dreamtime); Jackie Russell, Logan Murray, Doris Jones, R. M. Sanchez-Camus, Anna Micklefield, Suzanne Micklefield, Chahine Yavroyan, and Roxana Silbert; Beth Hardisty and Richard Rudnicki; Amelia Pimlott and Hannah Marshall (Ding Foundation); Jonty Roots, The Tapman, and Mr. Brutal; Fred Aylward, Molly Mathieson, and Conall Gleeson (New Note Orchestra); Karen Dawson, Rob Kennedy, Dan Thompson, Carpet Martin, Mayor Mark Greenhill, Christopher Trim, and Samantha Lindley (Threshold Studios); Seán Dagan Wood (*Positive News*); and the residents and staff of Penfold Community Hub and Ada Court. Also to Gaylene Gould and Vera Chok for sending me hopeful articles in the early days.

For their time, infinite patience, and expertise, my heartfelt and giant gratitude goes to all of my interviewees, including Charlotte Wiseman (Step Inside); Ben Hogbin (Discover Wellness); Tom Hart Dyke (Lullingstone Castle, designer of the World Garden of Plants); Marion Duggan (Clowns Without Borders); Cat Moon, Antonia Beck, and Lucy Nicholls (*The Death Show*); Damon Shaw; John Hindmarsh (Research Associate at Otto-Friedrich-Universität Bamberg); Paul Ardvison; David Harradine (Fevered Sleep); Natalie Russell and Ian Payton (NHS); George David Hodgson and Charlotte Hodgson (*Talkin' About* podcast); Moira Kerrane (Deptford Park Play Club); Trina Lynskey and Georgia Smith (DeptfordFolk); David Slater (Entelechy Arts); Malcolm and Deli (New Note Orchestra); Paul Prentice (Chaps Choir); Flick Ferdinando, Lizzie Dron, Gavin Hayes (Positive News); Seb Austin (Trees for Cities); Ronald Kiwalabye (Schools Trees Project); Suzanne Keyte, Lucy-Anne Holmes, Kathleen Towler, and Sarah Corbett (Craftivist Collective); Lachlan Joyner (Blue Mountains District RFS); Adam Bullock, Rebecca Cooper, Matt Hawkins, and Jennifer Nadel (Compassion in Politics); Thierry Spall, Mira Dovreni, Phillippe Spall, Rich Matthews, Jayne Nelson, and Evgenia Emets (Eternal Forest); Dr. Kimberley Trim (Imperial College London); Ashley James Brown; Dr. Dominic Galliano (University College London); Dr. Ashley Moyse, Tessa Buddle, Pyn Stockman, Testament, Adrian Gillott, Mandy Manners, and Kate Baily (Love Sober); Dominic Campbell (Creative Aging International); Natasha Khamjani (Folk Dance Remixed); Stella

Duffy OBE (co-director Fun Palaces); Dawn Atkinson (Evelyn Community Store); and Duncan Morrison, Nikki Jones, and Peter Culley (architect and founder of Spatial Affairs Bureau).

chapter notes

INTRODUCTION: IN SEARCH OF HOPE

Excerpt from Emily Dickinson's poem "'Hope' is the thing with feathers," from *The Poems of Emily Dickinson*, edited by R.W. Franklin (Harvard University Press, 1999)

Excerpt from *Thus Spoke Zarathustra* by Friedrich Nietzsche

Analysis about the 2011 UK riots can be found here: http://eprints.lse .ac.uk/46297/1/Reading%20the%20riots%28published%29.pdf

CHAPTER 1: ORDINARY DAYS

The Mary Jean Irion quote is from *Yes, world: a mosaic of meditation* (R. W. Baron Publishing, 1970)

Ben Hogbin and Discover Wellness can be found here: https://www .discoverwellness.co.uk

More about the Wellness Recovery Action Plan can be found here: https://mentalhealthrecovery.com

Watch U.S. Navy Admiral William H. McRaven speak about the importance of making your bed here: https://www.youtube.com /watch?v=pxBQLFLei70

Find out more about Charlotte Wiseman here: https:// charlottewiseman.com

Logan Murray's courses can be found here: http://loganmurray.com

The podcast with poet Maggie Smith can be found here: https://greatergood.berkeley.edu/podcasts/item/episode_49_how_to_find_your_silver_linings

CHAPTER 2: OUR YOUNGER SELVES

More information about Clowns Without Borders UK can be found here: https://www.clownswithoutborders.org.uk

Janet J. Boseovski's work can be found here: https://theconversation.com/children-are-natural-optimists-which-comes-with-psychological-pros-and-cons-93532

CHAPTER 3: HARD TIMES

Vanessa Woolf's work can be found here: https://www.londondreamtime.com

Vanessa's TEDx talk can be found here: https://www.youtube.com/watch?v=GTSyJIYGQoA&feature=emb_title

All about Tom Hart Dyke's garden: http://www.tomhartdyke.co.uk

Dr. Rick Hanson's work can be found here: https://www.rickhanson.net

The NHS Adult Psychiatric Morbidity Survey can be found via: https://digital.nhs.uk/data-and-information/publications/statistical/adult-psychiatric-morbidity-survey/adult-psychiatric-morbidity-survey-survey-of-mental-health-and-wellbeing-england-2014

Information from the National Alliance on Mental Illness (U.S.) can be found here: https://www.nami.org/mhstats

Information about the survey relating to suicide can be found here: https://www.nhs.uk/news/mental-health/uks-suicide-rate-highest -among-middle-aged-men/

Prince William discussing mental health van be found here: https:// www.youtube.com/watch?v=6_r58A2P71I

CHAPTER 4: FINDING THE LIGHT

Excerpt from Emily Dickinson's poem "That It Will Never Come Again" from *Emily Dickinson: The Complete Poems* (Faber and Faber, 1976)

The story of the well and the dragon is from Tolstoy's *My Confession* (1882)

British Social Attitudes surveys can be found here: https://www.bsa .natcen.ac.uk

The Religious Landscape Study can be found here: https://www .pewforum.org/religious-landscape-study/

The TV series *Cosmos* and Carl Sagan can be watched here: https:// www.youtube.com/watch?v=FT_nzxtgXEw

Information on *The Death Show* can be found here: http://the deathshow.co.uk

Candy Chang's projects can be found here: http://candychang.com

Ian Toothill's Everest story is here: https://www.bbc.co.uk/news/uk -england-south-yorkshire-42745531

Chahine Yavroyan's obituary can be read here: https://www.the guardian.com/stage/2018/nov/07/chahine-yavroyan-obituary

More about Fevered Sleep and This Grief Thing can be found here: https://www.feveredsleep.co.uk

The Good Grief Trust is here: https://www.thegoodgrieftrust.org

And Death Cafés here: https://deathcafe.com

CHAPTER 5: MURMURATIONS

Opening quote by Henry Melvill, from the sermon "Partaking in other Men's Sins" given at St. Margaret's Church, Lothbury, England on June 12, 1855. Printed in *Golden Lectures* (1855).

Matthew D. Lieberman's work I've referenced is from his book *Social: Why Our Brains Are Wired to Connect* (Oxford University Press, 2013)

The *Talkin' About* mental health podcast can be found on numerous podcast platforms, including Spotify and Apple Podcasts.

More about Octavia Hill can be found on the National Trust website: https://www.nationaltrust.org.uk

Information about Olaudah Equiano was from his autobiography, *The Interesting Narrative of the Life of Olaudah Equiano* (first published 1789)

For more about Thankfull Sturdee's work, read *Thankfull Sturdee: Deptford Photographer* by Sarah Crofts (Old Chapel Books, 2019). My research was done in Lewisham Library Archives.

For more about DeptfordFolk: https://www.deptfordfolk.org

More about Meet Me At: https://entelechyarts.org

And about the New Note Orchestra: https://www.newnote.co.uk

Grenfell United can be supported here: https://www.grenfellunited .org.uk

CHAPTER 6: THE EDGELANDS

Dr. Susanne Babbel talking about bad news and illness can be found here: https://edition.cnn.com/2018/06/01/health/bad-news-bad-health/index.html

The hundredth birthday story can be found here: https://www.goodhousekeeping.com/uk/news/a554785/lonely-elderly-winnie-100th-birthday-cards-radio-appeal-viral/

The story of Terrance and the choir can be found here: https://www.manchestereveningnews.co.uk/news/tv/bbc-breakfast-viewers-tears-oldham-17405352

The Some Good News YouTube channel can be found here: https://www.youtube.com/channel/UCOe_y6KKvS3PdIfb9q9pGug

Martyn Lewis speaking about positive news can be found here: https://www.youtube.com/watch?v=nfmfwUJswLA&list=UUPXVA29dh6o-2X08905TzhA&index=27

CHAPTER 7: DEEDS AND WORDS

The archive of the women's suffrage movement can be found via the London School of Economics: http://www.lse.ac.uk

Find out more about the No More Page Three campaign here: https://nomorepage3.wordpress.com/faqs/

Read about Kathleen Towler's campaign to save the woodland here: https://elflaw.org/past-cases/we-won-our-battle-to-save-ancient-woodland-on-the-hillcrest-estate-sydenham/

Sarah Corbett and the Craftivist Collective: https://craftivist-collective.com

A great source of information to help you support renewable energy is https://www.ethicalconsumer.org—with plenty of tips to help you "learn how to use your spending power to help change the world for the better."

The story of the Greensboro lunch counter is from *The Sit-Ins: Protest and Legal Change in the Civil Rights Era* by Christopher W. Schmidt (University of Chicago Press, 2018)

Find out more about the anti-apartheid movement in South Africa by reading *Long Walk to Freedom* by Nelson Mandela (Little, Brown and Company, 1994)

And more about Prague and the Velvet Revolution in *Disturbing the Peace* by Václav Havel (Vintage Books, 1990)

Watch all the young activists at Davos in 2020 here: https://www.youtube.com/watch?v=84pSP8CIhYM

Jacinda Ardern's speech at the General Assembly of the United Nations in 2019 can be seen here: https://www.youtube.com/watch?v=_we9agoBqyo

Compassion in Politics can be found here: https://www.compassioninpolitics.com

CHAPTER 8: HOPE IS A FOREST

Opening Shakespeare quote is from *Troilus and Cressida*, act 3, sc. 3.

You can read and see Greta Thunberg's address to the World Economic Forum in Davos 2019 here: https://www.weforum.org/agenda/2020/01/greta-thunberg-davos-message-climate-change/

Climate Scientists and reducing greenhouse gas emissions: https://
www.theguardian.com/environment/2019/sep/19/power-halve
-greenhouse-gas-emissions-2030-climate-scientists

John-Paul Flintoff's book *How to Change the World* (Macmillan, 2012)
can be found here: https://www.theschooloflife.com/london/

An interesting article about "eco-anxiety" and the work of Caroline
Hickman and others is here: https://time.com/5735388/climate
-change-eco-anxiety/

An interview with philosopher Edgar Morin can be found here: https://
news.cnrs.fr/articles/uncertainty-is-intrinsic-to-the-human-condition

The report on the view of the Himalayas in Jalandhar, India, can
be found here: https://edition.cnn.com/travel/article/himalayas
-visible-lockdown-india-scli-intl/index.html

Extinction Rebellion information was sourced from here: https://
rebellion.earth

The speech about love and grief by Gail Bradbrook: https://www
.newyorker.com/news/letter-from-the-uk/does-extinction
-rebellion-have-the-solution-to-the-climate-crisis

The global climate strikes: https://globalclimatestrike.net

Trees for Cities: https://www.treesforcities.org

A beginner's guide to planting trees in your own backyard can be
found here: https://www.countryliving.com/gardening/garden-ideas
/g29814701/trees-for-small-gardens/

The Schools Trees Project: https://www.givingway.com/organization
/child-care-foundation-schools-tree-project

One Tree Planted: https://onetreeplanted.org

American Forests: https://www.americanforests.org

For more information on the worldwide tree-planting projects, visit https://tree-nation.com/projects or https://blog.ecosia.org/tag /projects/ or https://www.trilliontreecampaign.org/donate-trees

Information about the Green Belt Movement can be found here: http://www.greenbeltmovement.org

The source of ideas for helping the rain forest can be found here: https://www.ran.org

Companies responsible for most carbon emissions: https://www.the guardian.com/sustainable-business/2017/jul/10/100-fossil-fuel-companies -investors-responsible-71-global-emissions-cdp-study-climate-change

Article about the Australian bushfires of 2019/2020 from the UN: https://www.unenvironment.org/news-and-stories/story/ten-impacts -australian-bushfires

Mayor Mark Greenhill's speech can be found on the Blue Mountain Firewatch Facebook page: https://www.facebook.com/groups /BlueMountainsFirewatch/

You can watch Jacinda Ardern's speech here: https://www.newshub .co.nz/home/politics/2019/11/historic-moment-mps-erupt-in -applause-as-zero-carbon-bill-passes-final-reading.html

CHAPTER 9: BACK TO THE FUTURE

Panorama's episode "Apollo 11: The Impact on Earth" was added to BBC iPlayer in 2014 and at the time of writing is still available there.

Tomorrowland is directed by Brad Bird and stars George Clooney. It was made in 2015 and is still widely available.

The utopian vision of *Star Trek* is discussed here: https://www.space.com

The PEW Research work about pessimism and the future can be found here: https://www.pewresearch.org/fact-tank/2019/03/21/looking-ahead-to-2050-americans-are-pessimistic-about-many-aspects-of-life-in-u-s/

The documentary *Plastic Fantastic*, presented by Mark Miodownik, can be found on BBC Radio 4 here: https://www.bbc.co.uk/programs/b0b450ls

Information on ocean plastic pollution and what's being done about it can be found here: https://theoceancleanup.com

More about Evoware can be found here: https://www.thejakartapost.com/life/2017/12/18/indonesian-startup-goes-eco-friendly-with-edible-cup.html

Some other solutions to plastic crisis can be found here: https://www.bbcearth.com/blog/?article=unexpected-solutions-to-the-plastic-crisis

Information about Eleos and Care(less): https://frequency.org.uk

About Ashley James Brown: https://ashleyjamesbrown.com

Threshold Studios: http://thresholdstudios.tv

And the Empathy Museum: http://www.empathymuseum.com

Innovation in dementia support: https://www.alzheimers.org.uk/blog/5-new-technologies-could-help-people-dementia-live-home-longer

For more about "food out of thin air": https://solarfoods.fi

About vertical farms coming to Washington, etc.: https://www.citylab
.com/life/2019/12/vertical-farming-local-food-grocery-stores
-infarm-plants/603457/

Eco-agriculture in Mali: https://farmingfirst.org/2016/06/eco-agriculture
-in-the-sahel/

Swillington Organic Farm: https://swillingtonorganicfarm.co.uk

"Agriculture at a Crossroads" can be found here: https://www.global
agriculture.org/fileadmin/files/weltagrarbericht/EnglishBrochure
/BrochureIAASTD_en_web_small.pdf

About Ron Finley, the "Gangsta Gardener": http://ronfinley.com

Watch Ron's TED talk here: https://www.ted.com/talks/ron_finley_a
_guerrilla_gardener_in_south_central_la?language=en

Article about free public transport in cities: https://www.forbes.com
/sitesc/enriquedans/2019/09/15/is-free-public-transport-in-cities
-the-wayforward/

Car-free Spain: https://www.theguardian.com/cities/2018/sep/18/paradise
-life-spanish-city-banned-cars-pontevedra

Solar power in Bangladesh: https://blogs.worldbank.org/climatechange
/lighting-rural-bangladesh-rooftop-solar-carbon-credits

Renewables in Wales: https://www.goodenergy.co.uk/blog/2017/11
/09/taff-bargoed-hydro/

Information about Taka Taka can be found here: https://takataka
solutions.com

a directory of hope

This is by no means a comprehensive list—more of a starter kit of publications, books, and other resources to help you in your quest to find and to keep hold of hope, in addition to those already mentioned in the chapter notes.

BOOKS

The Cloud Garden by Tom Hart Dyke and Paul Winder

Active Hope by Chris Johnstone and Joanna Macy

Hope in the Dark by Rebecca Solnit

A More Beautiful World Our Hearts Know Is Possible by Charles
     Eisenstein

A New Map of Wonders: A Journey in Search of Modern Marvels by
     Caspar Henderson

Yes to Life In Spite of Everything by Viktor E. Frankl

A Testament of Hope by Martin Luther King Jr.

Optimism over Despair by Noam Chomsky

Humankind: A Hopeful History by Rutger Bregman

Wellness Recovery Action Plan by Mary Ellen Copeland

No One Is Too Small to Make a Difference by Greta Thunberg

Our Future: How Kids Are Taking Action by Janet Wilson

Rise Up Women! by Dr. Diane Atkinson

Book of Play by Michael Rosen

How to Read a Protest by L. A. Kauffman

Flatpack Democracy by Peter Macfadyen

Winning the Green New Deal, edited by Varshini Prakash and
    Guido Girgenti

How to Be a Craftivist by Sarah Corbett

What Has Nature Ever Done for Us? by Tony Juniper

The World We Made by Jonathon Porritt

PODCASTS

How to Be Hopeful (everything to do with hope, hosted by me):
    https://whiterabbitpresents.podbean.com

Reasons to Be Cheerful (good news, hosted by Ed Miliband and
    Geoff Lloyd): https://www.cheerfulpodcast.com

Love Sober (self-care and recovery, hosted by Kate Baily and
    Mandy Manners): https://lovesober.podbean.com

The Science of Happiness (science and self-care, hosted by
    Dacher Keltner): https://greatergood.berkeley.edu
    /podcasts

The Infinite Monkey Cage (a witty look at the world from a scientist's perspective, hosted by Brian Cox and Robert Ince): https://www.bbc.co.uk/

Mothers of Invention (feminist solutions to climate change, hosted by former Irish president Mary Robinson and comedian Maeve Higgins): https://www.mothersof invention.online

OTHER RESOURCES

Tree People: https://www.treepeople.org

Black Lives Matter: https://blacklivesmatter.com/

Action for Happiness: https://www.actionforhappiness.org

The Optimist Daily: https://www.optimistdaily.com

Good News Network: https://www.goodnewsnetwork.org

The Happy Newspaper: https://thehappynewspaper.com

Tortoise: https://www.tortoisemedia.com

Positive News: https://www.positive.news

Reasons to be Cheerful: https://reasonstobecheerful.world

Good News Shared: https://goodnewsshared.com

New Scientist: https://www.newscientist.com

Great Good Science Center: https://greatergood.berkeley.edu

Brain Pickings (Maria Popova): https://www.brainpickings.org

2040: a documentary by Damon Gameau (also see https:// whatsyour2040.com for inspiring ideas)

A fantastic project called Homemade Mutant Hope Machines about "how people without much clout can start to build better worlds on their own terms" can be found at www.duckie.co.uk/drduckie

index

good, 65
grief, 77–81
illness/suffering, 72–77
lack of preparation for, 62–63
pandemic and, 62
preparation for, 65–67
science and, 60–61
talking about, 66–67, 72
things to do before, 68–69
wild hope and, 79–80
Death Cafés, 81
Death Show, The (theater show), 63–65,
67, 71
deforestation, 169. *See also* climate
change; tree planting
dementia, 188–189
depression, 49. *See also* mental health
DeptfordFolk, 93
despair, 39–58
Dickinson, Emily, 59
disappointment, as chance to learn
and grow, 25–26
Discover Wellness, 7–10
dopamine, 35, 89, 136
Doyle, Trish, 173
dreams, acting on, 19–20
Dubs, Lord, 147
Duggan, Marion, 32–33

E

eco-agriculture, 191–192
Edgelands, 110–123
Edison, Thomas, 18
Einstein, Albert, 183
elected officials
climate change and, 171–174
positive actions and, 144–149
Eleos, 187–188
empathy, 188, 189
Empathy Jacket, 188
Empathy Museum, 188
end-of-life care, 65
environment. *See also* climate change;
nature

pandemic and, 155
plastic and, 183–185
Equiano, Olaudah, 91
everyday
everyday beauty, 3–4
finding hope in, 1–21
Evoware, 185
Extinction Rebellion protest, 159–160

F

failure, reframing, 18–20
faith, 60, 62
Fawcett, Millicent, 127
fear, 49. *See also* mental health
constant exposure to, 109
responding to, 109, 136
"fight, flight, or freeze" response, 109, 136
Finding Silver Linings, 16–17
Finley, Ron, 192
Flintoff, John-Paul, 153
flow, 7, 29
food, 189–193
future
fears about, 186
finding hope for, 176–196
looking forward to, 57
optimism about, 178–180
pessimism about, 181–182
technology and, 187–189

G

game night, 33
goal setting, 45–46
goals, little, 10–11
Gómez-Colón, Salvador, 142
governments
climate change and, 171–174
positive actions and, 144–149
Greater Good Science Center, 16–17
Green Belt Movement, 167
Green Corps, 166
Greenhill, Mark, 172, 173
Grenfell Tower fire, 102–103

about the author

Bernadette Russell is an author, storyteller, performer, and activist. She has been a columnist for *Balance* magazine since 2016, and her previous books include *The Little Book of Kindness* and *The Little Book of Wonder*. She has written on the subject of hope and kindness for many other publications, including *The Guardian, Daily Express, Daily Mirror*, and the *Daily Telegraph*. Since 2012, she has toured the U.S. and UK speaking about the importance and life-changing experience of practicing kindness, including for Talk Radio, BBC Radio 4 Saturday Live, Action for Happiness, Birmingham School of Philosophy, and the Southbank Center, where she was nominated as one of sixty-seven change makers for her project 366 Days of Kindness.

Bernadette presents the *How to be Hopeful* podcast, which can be found at http://whiterabbitpresents.podbean.com.

More information can be found on Instagram @bernadetterussell, on Twitter @betterussell, or online at bernadetterussell.com.